Music Notation and Terminology

By

Karl W. Gehrkens

Cover Photograph: Brandon Giesbrecht

ISBN: 978-1-84902-273-6

PREFACE

The study of *music notation and terminology* by classes in conservatories and in music departments of colleges and normal schools is a comparative innovation, one reason for the non-existence of such courses in the past being the lack of a suitable text-book, in which might be found in related groups clear and accurate definitions of the really essential terms. But with the constantly increasing interest in music study (both private and in the public schools), and with the present persistent demand that music teaching shall become more systematic and therefore more efficient in turning out a more *intelligent* class of pupils, it has become increasingly necessary to establish courses in which the prospective teacher of music (after having had considerable experience with music itself) might acquire a concise and accurate knowledge of a fairly large number of terms, most of which he has probably already encountered as a student, and many of which he knows the general meaning of, but none of which he perhaps knows accurately enough to enable him to impart his knowledge clearly and economically to others.

To meet the need of a text-book for this purpose in his own classes the author has been for several years gathering material from all available sources, and it is hoped that the arrangement of this material in related groups as here presented will serve to give the student not only some insight into the present meaning of a goodly number of terms, but will also enable him to see more clearly *why* certain terms have the meaning which at present attaches to them. To this latter end the derivations of many of the terms are given in connection with their definition.

The aim has not been to present an exhaustive list, and the selection of terms has of course been influenced largely by the author's own individual experience, hence many teachers will probably feel that important terms have been omitted that should have been included. For this state of affairs no apology is offered except that it would probably be impossible to write a book on this subject which would satisfy everyone in either the selection or actual definition of terms.

In formulating the definitions themselves an attempt has been made to use such words as *note, tone,* et cetera with at least a fair degree of accuracy, and while the attitude of the author on this point may be criticized as being puristic and pedantic, it is nevertheless his opinion that the next generation of music students and teachers will be profited by a more accurate use of certain terms that have been inaccurately used for so long that the present generation has to a large extent lost sight of the fact that the use is inaccurate. The author is well aware of the fact that reform is a matter of growth rather than of edict, but he is also of the belief that before reform can actually begin to come, the *need* of reform must be felt by a fairly large number of actively interested persons. It is precisely because so few musicians realize the need of any change in music terminology that the changes recommended by committees who have given the matter careful thought are so slow in being adopted. It is hoped that some few points at which reform in the terminology of music is necessary may be brought to the attention of a few additional musicians thru this volume, and that the cause may thus be helped in some slight degree.

It is suggested that in using the book for class-room purposes the teacher emphasize not only the definition and derivation of all terms studied, but the spelling and pronunciation as well. For this latter purpose a pronouncing index has been appended.

It is impossible to give credit to all sources from which ideas have been drawn, but especial mention should be made of the eminently clear and beautifully worded definitions compiled by Professor Waldo S. Pratt for the Century Dictionary, and the exceedingly valuable articles on an almost all-inclusive range of topics found in the new edition of Grove's Dictionary. Especial thanks for valuable suggestions as to the arrangement of the material, etc., are also due to Dr. Raymond H. Stetson, Professor of Psychology, Oberlin College; Arthur E. Heacox, Professor of Theory, Oberlin Conservatory of Music; and Charles I. Rice, Supervisor of Music, Worcester, Mass., as well as to various members of the Music Teachers' National Association who have offered valuable advice along certain specific lines.

K. W. G.

OBERLIN CONSERVATORY OF MUSIC,
June, 1913

CONTENTS

CONTENTS

CHAPTER I

Some Principles of Correct Notation

1. The *note* (from *nota* — Latin — a mark or sign) consists of either one, two, or three parts, (𝅝 𝅘𝅥 𝅘𝅥𝅮) these being referred to respectively as head, stem, and hook. The hook is often called *tail* or cross-stroke. The stem appears on the right side of the head when turned up, but on the left side when turned down.[1] 𝅘𝅥 𝅘𝅥 The hook is always on the right side.[2] 𝅘𝅥𝅮 𝅘𝅥𝅮

In writing music with pen the head and hook are best made with a heavy pressure on the pen point, but in writing at the board they are most easily made by using a piece of chalk about an inch long, turned on its side.

2. When only one part (or voice) is written on the staff, the following *rules for turning stems* apply: (1) If the note-head is *below* the third line, the stem must turn up. (2) If the note-head is *above* the third line the stem must turn down. (3) If the note-head is *on* the third line the stem is turned either up or down with due regard to the symmetrical appearance of the measure in which the note occurs. The following examples will illustrate these points.

Fig. 1.

---

[1] It should be noted at the outset that this statement regarding the down-turned stem on the left side of the note-head, and also a number of similar principles here cited, refer more specifically to music as it appears on the printed page. In the case of hand-copied music the down-turned stem appears on the right side of the note, thus 𝅘𝅥.
This is done because of greater facility in writing, and for the same reason other slight modifications of the notation here recommended may sometimes be encountered. In dealing with children it is best usually to follow as closely as possible the principles according to which *printed* music is notated, in order to avoid those non-satisfying and often embarassing explanations of differences which will otherwise be unavoidable.
[2] An exception to this rule occurs in the case of notes of unequal value stroked together, when the hook appears on the left side, thus 𝅘𝅥𝅮𝅘𝅥.

3. When two parts are written on the same staff, the stems of the upper part all turn up, and those of the lower part turn down, in order that the parts may be clearly distinguished. (Fig. 2.) But in music for piano and other instruments on which complete chords can be sounded by *one* performer and also in simple, four-part vocal music in which all voices have approximately the same rhythm, several notes often have one stem in common as in Fig. 3.

Fig. 3.

Fig. 2.

4. Notes of small denomination (eighths and smaller) are often written in groups of two or more, all stems in the group being then connected by *one cross-stroke*. In such a case all the stems must of course be turned the same way, the direction being determined by the position of the majority of note-heads in the group. Notes thus *stroked* may be of the same or of different denomination. See Fig. 4.

Fig. 4.

In vocal music notes are never thus stroked when a syllable is given to each note. (See p. 19, Sec. 55, C.)

5. *Rests*, like notes, are best made with a heavy pen stroke or by using a piece of chalk on its side. (See note under Sec. 1.) The double-whole rest, whole rest, and half rest occupy the third space unless for the sake of clearness in writing two parts on the same staff they are written higher or lower. The rests of smaller denomination may be placed at any point on the staff, the hooks being always placed on the spaces. The hook

of the eighth rest is usually placed on the *third* space.   Rests are sometimes dotted, but are never tied.

6. The *G clef* should be begun at the second line rather than below the staff.   Experiments have shown clearly that beginners learn to make it most easily in this way, and the process may be further simplified by dividing it into two parts, thus, ⎇ |.   The descending stroke crosses the ascending curve at or near the fourth line.   The circular part of the curve occupies approximately the first and second spaces.

7. The *F clef* is made either thus, 𝄢, or, thus, 𝄢, the dots being placed one on either side of the fourth line of the staff, which is the particular point that the clef marks.   The C *clef* has also two forms, ‖≡‖ and 𝄡.

8. The *sharp* is made with two light vertical strokes, and two heavy slanting ones, the slant of the latter being upward from left to right, ♯.   The sharp should never be made thus, ♯.

The *double sharp* is made either thus × or ＊, the first form being at present the more common.

9. The *flat* is best made by a down stroke retraced part way up, the curve being made without lifting pen from paper.   The *double flat* consists of two flats,[1] ♭♭.   The *natural* or *cancel* is made in two strokes, down-right and right-down, thus ♮ ♮ ♮.

10. The *tie* usually connects the *heads* of notes, thus ♩ ♩.

11. The *dot after a note* always appears on a space, whether the note-head is on a line or space.   (See Fig. 5.)   In the case of a dot after a note on a line, the dot usually appears on the space *above* that line if the next note is higher in position and on the space below it if the following note is lower.

---

[1] It is to be hoped that the figure for the double-flat suggested by Mattheson (who also suggested the St. Andrew's cross (✕) for the double-sharp) may some time be readopted.   This figure was the Greek letter B, made thus, β, and its use would make our notation one degree more uniform than it is at present.

Fig. 5.

Note. — Correct notation must be made a habit rather than a theory, and in order to form the habit of writing correctly, *drill* is necessary. This may perhaps be best secured by asking students to write (at the board or on ruled paper) from verbal dictation, thus: Teacher says,

"Key of B♭, three-quarter measure: First measure, DO a quarter note, RE a quarter, and Mi a quarter. Second measure, SOL a quarter, LA a quarter, and SOL a quarter. Third measure, LA, TI, DO, RE, MI, RE, eighths, stroked in pairs. Fourth measure, high DO a dotted half." Pupils respond by writing the exercise dictated, after which mistakes in the turning of stems, etc., are corrected. The *pitch names* may be dictated instead of the syllables if desired, and still further practice may be provided by asking that the exercise be transposed to other keys.

CHAPTER II

Symbols of Music Defined

12. A *staff* is a collection of parallel lines, together with the spaces belonging to them. The modern staff has five lines and six spaces, these being ordinarily referred to as first line, second line, third line, fourth line, and fifth line (beginning with the lowest); and space below (*i.e.*, space below the first line), first space, second space, third space, fourth space, and space above.

The definition and discussion above refer more specifically to one of the portions of the "great staff," the latter term being often applied to the combination of treble and bass staffs (with one leger line between) so commonly used in piano music, etc.

13. The *extent of the staff* may be increased either above or below by the addition of short lines called *leger lines*,[1] and notes may be written on either these lines or on the spaces above and below them.

14. The lines and spaces constituting the staff (including leger lines if any) are often referred to as *staff degrees*, *i.e.*, each separate line and space is considered to be "a degree of the staff." The tones of a scale are also sometimes referred to as "degrees of the scale."

15. A *clef*[2] is a sign placed on the staff to designate what pitches are to be represented by its lines and spaces. Thus, *e.g.*, the G clef shows us not only that the second line of the staff represents G, but that the first line represents E, the first space F, etc. The F clef similarly shows us that the fifth line

---

[1] The word *leger* is derived from the French word *LÉGER*, meaning light, and this use of the word refers to the fact that the leger lines, being added by hand, are lighter — *i.e.*, less solid in color — than the printed lines of the staff itself.

[2] The word *clef* is derived from *CLAVIS* — a key — the reference being to the fact that the clef unlocks or makes clear the meaning of the staff, as a key to a puzzle enables us to solve the puzzle.

of the bass staff represents the first A below middle C, the fourth line the first F below middle C, etc.

The student should note that these clefs are merely modified forms of the letters G and F, which (among others) were used to designate the pitches represented by certain lines when staff notation was first inaugurated. For a fuller discussion of this matter see Appendix A, p. 101.

16. When the G clef is used the staff is usually referred to as the *treble staff*, and when the F clef is used, as the *bass staff*. Such expressions as "singing from the treble clef," or "singing in the treble clef," and "singing in the bass clef" are still frequently heard, but are preferably replaced by "singing from the treble staff," and "singing from the bass staff." Fig. 6 shows the permanent names of lines and spaces when the G and F clefs are used.[1]

Fig. 6.

17. *The movable C clef* ▤ or ▥, formerly in very common use, is now utilized for only two purposes, viz., (1) in music written for certain orchestral instruments (cello, viola, etc.) of extended range, in order to avoid having to use too many leger lines; and (2) for indicating the tenor part in vocal music. This latter usage seems also to be disappearing however, and the tenor part is commonly written on the treble staff, it being understood that the tones are to be sung an octave lower than the notes would indicate.

---

[1] The Germans use the same pitch designations as we do with two exceptions, viz., our B is called by them H, and our B♭ is called B. The scale of C therefore reads: C, D, E, F, G, A, H, C; the scale of F reads F, G, A, B, C, D, E, F. The signatures are in all cases written exactly as we write them.

In France and Italy where the "fixed DO" system is in vogue, pitches are usually referred to by the syllable names; *e.g.*, C is referred to as DO (or UT), D as RE, etc.

The C clef as used in its various positions is shown in Figs. 7, 8, and 9. It will be noted that in each case the line on which the clef is placed represents "middle C."

Fig. 7.	**Fig. 8.**	**Fig. 9.**
Soprano clef.	Alto clef.	Tenor clef.

18. A *sharp* is a character that causes any degree of the staff on which it is placed or with which it is associated to represent a pitch one half-step higher than it otherwise would.

Thus in Fig. 10 (a) the fifth line and first space represent the pitch F, but in Fig. 10 (b) these same staff degrees represent an entirely different tone — F♯. The student should note that the sharp does not then *raise* anything ; it merely causes a staff degree to represent a higher tone than it otherwise would. There is just as much difference between F and F♯ as between B and C, and yet one would never think of referring to C as "B raised"!

Fig. 10.

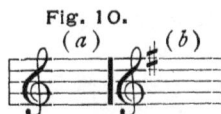

19. A *flat* is a character that causes any degree of the staff on which it is placed or with which it is associated to represent a pitch one half-step lower than it otherwise would. (See note under section 18 above and apply the same discussion here.)

20. A *double-sharp* causes the staff degree on which it is placed to represent a pitch one whole-step higher than it would without any sharp. Similarly, a double-flat causes the staff degree on which it is placed to represent a pitch one whole-step lower than it would without any flat.

Double-sharps and double-flats are generally used on staff degrees that have already been sharped or flatted, therefore their practical effect is to cause staff degrees to represent pitches respectively a half-step higher and a half-step lower than would be represented by those same degrees in their diatonic condition. Thus in Fig. 10 (b) the first space in its diatonic condition [1] represents F-sharp, and the double-sharp on this degree would cause it to represent a pitch one-half step higher than F-sharp, *i.e.*, F-double-sharp.

---

[1] The expression "diatonic condition" as here used refers to the staff after the signature has been placed upon it, in other words after the staff has been prepared to represent the pitches of the diatonic scale.

CHAPTER III

Symbols of Music Defined (*Continued*)

21. The *natural*[1] (sometimes called *cancel*) annuls the effect of previous sharps, flats, double-sharps, and double-flats, within the measure in which it occurs. After a double-sharp or double-flat the combination of a natural with a sharp, or a natural with a flat is often found: in this case only one sharp or flat is annulled. (Sometimes also the single sharp or flat will be found by itself, cancelling the double-sharp or double-flat). The natural is often used when a composition changes key, as in Fig. 11, where a change from E to G is shown.

Fig. 11.

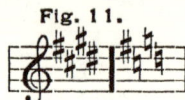

22. The group of sharps or flats (or absence of them) at the beginning of a staff partially indicates the key in which the composition is written. They are called collectively the *key-signature*.

23. The same key-signature may stand for either one of two keys, the major key, or its relative minor, hence in order to determine in what key a melody is one must note whether the tones are grouped about the major tonic DO or the minor tonic LA. In a harmonized composition it is almost always possible to determine the key by referring to the last bass note; if the final chord is clearly the DO chord the composition is in the major key, but if this final chord is clearly the LA chord then it is almost certain that the entire composition is in the

---

[1] It has already been noted (p. 6, **Note**) that in the German scale our b-flat is called b, and our b is called H. From this difference in terminology has grown up the custom of using the H (now made ♮) to show that *any* staff-degree is in *natural* condition, *i.e.*, not sharped or flatted.

minor key. Thus if a final chord appears as that in Fig. 12 the composition is clearly in G major, while if it appears as in Fig. 13, it is just as surely in E minor.

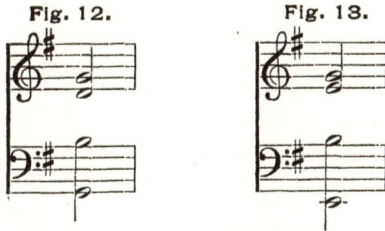

Fig. 12.

Fig. 13.

24. Sharps, flats, naturals, double-sharps and double-flats, occurring in the course of the composition (*i.e.*, after the key signature) are called *accidentals*, whether they actually cause a staff degree to represent a different pitch as in Fig. 14 or simply make clear a notation about which there might otherwise be some doubt as in Fig. 15, measure two. The effect of such accidentals terminates at the bar.

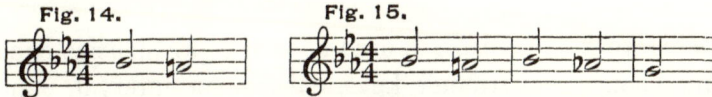

Fig. 14.

Fig. 15.

25. In the case of a *tie across a bar* an accidental remains in force until the combined value of the tied notes expires. In Fig. 16 first measure, third beat, an accidental sharp makes the third space represent the pitch C sharp. By virtue of the tie across the bar the third space continues to represent C sharp thru the first beat of the second measure, but for the remainder of the measure the third space will represent C unless the sharp is repeated as in Fig. 17.

Fig. 16.

Fig. 17.

26. The following rules for making staff degrees represent pitches different from those of the diatonic scale will be found useful by the beginner in the study of music notation. These

rules are quoted from "The Worcester Musical Manual," by
Charles I. Rice.

1. To sharp a natural degree, use a sharp.   Fig. 18.
2. To sharp a sharped degree, use a double sharp.   Fig. 19.
3. To sharp a flatted degree, use a natural.   Fig. 20.
4. To flat a natural degree, use a flat.   Fig. 21.
5. To flat a flatted degree, use a double flat.   Fig. 22.
6. To flat a sharped degree, use a natural.   Fig. 23.

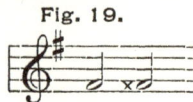

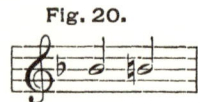

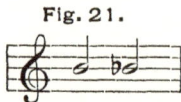

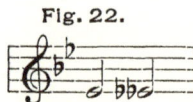

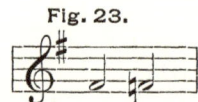

Fig. 18.   **Fig. 19.**   **Fig. 20.**

Fig. 21.   **Fig. 22.**   **Fig. 23.**

27. When two different notations represent the same pitch,
the word *enharmonic* is applied.   Thus we may say that F
sharp and G flat (on keyboard instruments at least) are enharmonically the same.

This word *enharmonic* is used in such expressions as enharmonic change, enharmonic keys, enharmonic interval, enharmonic modulation, enharmonic relation, etc., and in all such
combinations it has the same meaning, viz. — a change in
notation but no change in the pitch represented.

28. A *note* is a character expressing relative duration,
which when placed on a staff indicates that a certain tone is to
be sounded for a certain relative length of time.   The pitch of
the tone to be sounded is shown by the position of the note on
the staff, while the length of time it is to be prolonged is shown
by the shape of the note.   Thus *e.g.*, a half-note on the second
line of the treble staff indicates that a specific pitch (g′) is to be
played or sung for a period of time twice as long as would be
indicated by a quarter-note in the same composition.

29. A *rest* is a character which indicates a rhythmic silence
of a certain relative length.

30. The *notes and rests in common use* are as follows:

Whole-note.   An open note-head without stem.

Half-note.   An open note-head with stem.

Quarter-note.   A closed note-head with stem.

Eighth-note.   A closed note-head with stem and one hook.

Sixteenth-note.   A closed note-head with stem and two hooks.

Thirty-second-note.   A closed note-head with stem and three hooks.

Whole-rest.

Half-rest.

Quarter-rest.

Eighth-rest.

Sixteenth-rest.

Thirty-second-rest.

31. The *English names* for these notes are:

Whole-note — semi-breve.
Half-note — minim.
Quarter-note — crotchet.
Eighth-note — quaver.
Sixteenth-note — semi-quaver.
Thirty-second-note — demi-semi-quaver.

The corresponding rests are referred to by the same system of nomenclature: *e.g., semi-breve rest,* etc.

32. *Sixty-fourth* and *one-hundred-and-twenty-eighth-notes* are occasionally found, but are not in common use. The *double-whole-note* (*breve*), made ‖○‖ or ▬, is still used, especially in English music, which frequently employs the half-note as the beat-unit. Thus in four-half measure the breve would be necessary to indicate a tone having four beats.

. 33. The *whole-rest* has a peculiarity of usage not common to any of the other duration symbols, viz., that it is often employed as a *measure-rest,* filling an entire measure of beats, no matter what the measure-signature may be. Thus, not only in four-quarter-measure, but in two-quarter, three-quarter, six-eighth, and other varieties, the whole-rest fills the entire measure, having a value sometimes greater, sometimes less than the corresponding whole-note. Because of this peculiarity of usage the whole-rest is termed *Takt-pausa* (measure-rest) by the Germans.

34. A *bar* is a vertical line across the staff, dividing it into measures. The word *bar* is often used synonymously with *measure* by orchestral conductors and others; thus, "begin at the fourteenth bar after J." This use of the word, although popular, is incorrect.

35. A *double-bar* consists of two vertical lines across the staff, at least one of the two being a heavy line. The double bar marks the end of a division, movement, or entire composition.

CHAPTER IV

ABBREVIATIONS, SIGNS, ETC.

36. A *double bar* (or single heavy bar) with either two or four dots indicates that a section is to be repeated. If the repeat marks occur at only one point the entire preceding part is to be repeated, but if the marks occur twice (the first time at the right of the bar but the second time at the left), only the section thus enclosed by the marks is to be repeated.

37. Sometimes a different cadence (or ending) is to be used for the repetition, and this is indicated as in Fig. 24.

Fig. 24.

38. The Latin word *bis* is occasionally used to indicate that a certain passage or section is to be repeated. This use is becoming obsolete.

39. The words *da capo* (*D.C.*) mean literally "from the head," *i.e.*, repeat from the beginning. The words *dal segno* (*D.S.*) indicate a repetition from the sign (:S: or 𝄋) instead of from the beginning.

In the case of both *D.C.* and *D.S.* the word *fine* (meaning literally *the end*) is ordinarily used to designate the point at which the repeated section is to terminate. The fermata (⌢) was formerly in common use for this same purpose, but is seldom so employed at present.

D.C. (*sin*[1]) *al fine* means — repeat from the beginning to the word "fine."

D.C. al ⌒ means — repeat to the fermata (or hold).

D.C. senza repetitione, or *D.C. ma senza repetitione,* both mean — repeat from the beginning, but without observing other repeat marks during the repetition.

D.C. e poi la coda means — repeat the first section only to the mark ⨁, then skip to the coda. (See p. 74, Sec. 157, for discussion of *coda*).

40. In certain cases where the repetition of characteristic figures can be indicated without causing confusion, it is the practice of composers (especially in orchestral music) to make use of certain *signs of repetition.* Some of the commonest of these abbreviations are shown in the following examples.

Fig. 25.   Written   Played   Fig. 26.   Written   Played

Fig. 27.   Written.   Played.

In Fig. 28 the repetition of an entire measure is called for.

Fig. 28.

41. The word *similie* (sometimes *segue*) indicates that a certain effect previously begun is to be continued, as *e.g.,* staccato playing, pedalling, style of bowing in violin music, etc. The word *segue* is also occasionally used to show that an accompaniment figure (especially in orchestral music) is to be continued.

42. *When some part is to rest for two or more measures* several methods of notation are possible. A rest of two measures is usually indicated thus ⊒⊏. Three measures thus ⊒⊏. Four measures thus ⊒⊏. Rests of more than

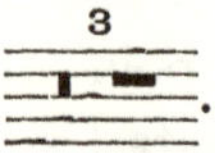

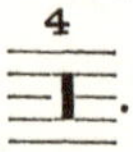

---

[1] The word *sin* is a contraction of the Italian word *sino,* meaning "as far as" or "until"; in the term given above (Sec. 39) it is really superfluous as the word *al* includes in itself both preposition and article, meaning "to the."

four measures are usually indicated in one of the following

ways· [musical notation] Sometimes the number of measures is written directly on the staff, thus; [musical notation with 8].

43. The letters G.P. (general pause, or grosse pause),the words *lunga pausa*, or simply the word *lunga*, **are** sometimes written over a rest to show that there is to be a prolonged pause or rest in all parts. Such expressions are found only in ensemble music, *i.e.*, music in which several performers are engaged at the same time.

44. The *fermata* or *hold* ⌢ over a note or chord indicates that the tone is to be prolonged, the duration of the prolongation depending upon the character of the music and the taste of the performer or conductor. It has already been noted that the hold over a bar was formerly used to designate the end of the composition, as the word *fine* is employed at present, but this usage has practically disappeared and the hold over the bar now usually indicates a short rest between two sections of a composition.

45. The sign *8va*...... (an abbreviation of *al ottava*, literally at the octave) above the staff, indicates that all tones are to be sounded an octave higher than the notes would indicate. When found below the staff the same sign serves to indicate that the tones are to be sounded an octave lower. The term *8va bassa* has also this latter signification.

46. Sometimes the word *loco* (in place) is used to show that the part is no longer to be sounded an octave higher (or lower), but this is more often indicated by the termination of the dotted (or wavy) line.

47. The sign *Col 8* (*col ottava* — with the octave) shows that the tones an octave higher or lower are to be sounded *with* the tones indicated by the printed notes.

48. For the sake of definiteness in referring to pitches, a specific name is applied to each octave, and all pitches in

the octave are referred to by means of a uniform nomenclature. The following figure will make this system clear:

Fig. 29.

Thus e.g., "great G" (written simply G), is the G represented by the first line of the bass staff. Small A (written a), is represented by the fifth line of the bass staff. Two-lined G, (written $\bar{\bar{g}}$), is represented by the space above the fifth line, treble staff. Three-lined C, (written $\bar{\bar{c}}$), is represented by the second added line above the treble staff, etc. The one-lined octave may be described as the octave from middle C to the B represented by the third line of the treble staff, and any tone within that octave is referred to as "one-lined." Thus — one-lined D, one-lined G, etc.

In scientific works on acoustics, etc., the pitches in the sub octave (or sub-contra octave as it is often called) are referred to as C_2, D_2, E_2, etc.; those in the contra octave as C_1, D_1, etc.; in the great octave, as c^1, d^1, etc.; in the small octave as c^2, d^2, etc.

CHAPTER V

ABBREVIATIONS, SIGNS, ETC., (*Continued*)

49. *A dot after a note* shows that the value of the note is to be half again as great as it would be without the dot, *i.e.*, the value is to be three-halves that of the original note.

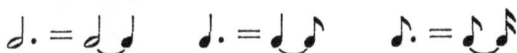

$$\text{♩.} = \text{♩}\text{♩} \qquad \text{♩.} = \text{♩}\text{♪} \qquad \text{♪.} = \text{♪}\text{♬}$$

50. *When two dots follow the note* the second dot adds half as much as the first dot has added, *i.e.*, the entire value is seven-fourths that of the original note.

$$\text{♩..} = \text{♩}\text{♪}\text{♬} \qquad \text{♩.} = \text{♩}\text{♪}\text{♬}$$

51. *When three dots follow the note* the third dot adds one-half the value added by the second, *i.e.*, the entire value of the triple-dotted note is fifteen-eighths that of the original note.

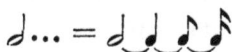

$$\text{♩...} = \text{♩}\text{♩}\text{♪}\text{♬}$$

52. *A dot over or under a note* is called the *staccato mark* and indicates that the tone is to be sounded and then instantly released. In music for organ and for some other instruments the staccato note is sometimes interpreted differently, this depending on the character of the instrument.

On stringed instruments of the violin family the staccato effect is usually secured by a long, rapid stroke of the bow for each tone; in the case of harp and drum the hand is quickly brought in contact with the vibrating body, thus stopping the tone instantly. On the organ the tone is often prolonged to one-half the value of the printed note before the keys are released.

53. *The wedge-shaped dash over the note* (staccatissimo) was formerly employed to indicate a tone still more detached

17

than that indicated by the dot, but this sign is really super-fluous, and is seldom used at present.

54. *A tie* is a curved line connecting the heads of two notes that call for the same tone. It indicates that but one tone is to be sounded, this tone having a duration equal to the combined value of both notes. *E.g.*, a half-note tied to a quarter-note would indicate a tone equal in duration-length to that shown by a dotted half-note; two half-notes tied would indicate a tone equal in duration to that shown by a whole-note. (See examples under Sections 49, 50, and 51).

Fig. 30 illustrates the more common variety of tie, while Fig. 31 shows an example of the *enharmonic*[1] *tie.* ·

Fig. 30.   Fig. 31.

55. The *slur* is used in so many different ways that it is impossible to give a general definition. It consists of a curved line, sometimes very short (in which case it looks like the tie), but sometimes very long, connecting ten, fifteen, or more notes. Some of the more common uses of the slur are:

A. *To indicate legato* (sustained or connected) *tones*, as contrasted with staccato (detached) ones.

In violin music this implies playing all tones thus slurred in one bow; in music for the voice and for wind instruments it implies singing or playing them in one breath.

B. *As a phrase-mark*, in the interpretation of which the first tone of the phrase is often accented slightly, and the last one shortened in value.

This interpretation of the phrase is especially common when the phrase is short (as in the two-note phrase), and when the tones constituting the phrase are of short duration, *e.g.*, the phrase given in Fig. 32 would be played approximately as written in Fig. 33.

Fig. 32.   Fig. 33.

etc.

[1] For definition of enharmonic see p. 10, Sec. 27.

But if the notes are of greater value, especially in slow tempi, the slur merely indicates legato, *i.e.*, sustained or connected rendition. Fig. 34 illustrates such a case.

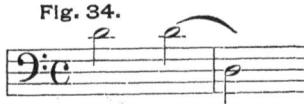

Fig. 34.

This is a matter of such diverse usage that it is difficult to generalize regarding it. The tendency seems at present to be in the direction of using the slur (*in instrumental music*) as a phrase-mark exclusively, it being understood that unless there is some direction to the contrary, the tones are to be performed in a connected manner.

C. In vocal music, to show that two or more tones are to be sung to one syllable of text. See Fig. 35.

Fig. 35.   MENDELSSOHN (*S. Paul*)

re - mem - bers His chil - dren.

In notes of small denomination (eighths and smaller) this same thing is often indicated by *stroking* the stems together as in Fig. 36. This can only be done in cases where the natural grouping of notes in the measure will not be destroyed.

Fig. 36.

ev - er and ev - er, for ev - er and

D. To mark special note-groups (triplets, etc.), in which case the slur is accompanied by a figure indicating the number of notes in the group. See Fig. 37 (*a*).

The most common of these irregular note-groups is the *triplet*, which consists of three notes to be performed in the time ordinarily given to two of the same value. Sometimes the triplet consists of only two notes as in Fig. 37 (*b*). In such a case the first two of the three notes composing the triplet are considered to be tied.

Fig. 37.

(*a*)   (*b*)   (*b*)

When the triplet form is perfectly obvious, the Fig. 3 (as well as the slur) may be omitted.

Other examples of irregular note-groups, together with the names commonly applied, follow.

Doublet	Quintuplet	Sextuplet	Septolet
	or	or	or
	Quintolet	Sextolet	Septimole

56. The *combination of slur or tie and dots* over the notes indicates that the tones are to be somewhat detached, but not

sharply so.

This effect is sometimes erroneously termed *portamento* (lit. *carrying*), but this term is more properly reserved for an entirely different effect, *viz.*, when a singer, or player on a stringed instrument, passes from a high tone to a low one (or vice versa) touching lightly on some or all of the diatonic tones between the two melody tones.

57. The horizontal *dash over a note* ⲡ indicates that the tone is to be slightly accented, and sustained. This mark is also sometimes used after a staccato passage to show that the tones are no longer to be performed in detached fashion, but are to be sustained. This latter use is especially common in music for stringed instruments.

58. The combination of *dash and dot over a note* ⲡ indicates that the tone is to be slightly accented and separated from its neighboring tones.

59. *Accent marks* are made in a variety of fashions. The most common forms follow.   ⟩ ∧ *sffz*. All indicate that a certain tone or chord is to be differentiated from its neighboring tones or chords by receiving a certain relative amount of stress.

60. In music for keyboard instruments it is sometimes necessary to indicate that a certain part is to be played by a certain hand. The abbreviations r.h. (right hand), m.d. (mano destra, It.), and m.d. (main droite, Fr.), designate that a passage or tone is to be played with the right hand, while l.h. (left hand), m.s. (mano sinistra, It.), and m.g. (main gauche, Fr.), show that the left hand is to be employed.

61. *The wavy line placed vertically beside a chord*

indicates that the tones are to be sounded consecutively instead of simultaneously, beginning with the lowest tone, all tones being sustained until the duration-value of the chord has expired. This is called *arpeggio playing*. When the wavy line extends through the entire chord (covering both staffs) as in Fig. 38, all the tones of the chord are to be played one after another, beginning with the lowest: but if there is a separate wavy line for each staff as at Fig. 39 then the lowest tone represented on the upper staff is to be played simultaneously with the lowest tone represented on the bass staff.

Fig. 38.   Fig. 39.

Written   Played

The word arpeggio (plural arpeggi) is a derivation of the Italian word *arpa* (meaning harp), and from this word *arpa* and its corresponding verb *arpeggiare* (to play on the harp) are derived also a number of other terms commonly used in instrumental music. Among these are — arpeggiamento, arpeggiando, arpeggiato, etc., all of these terms referring to a *harp style* of performance, the tones being sounded one after another in rapid succession instead of simultaneously as on the piano.

62. The sign ⟨⟩ over a note indicates that the tone is to be begun softly, gradually increased in power, and as gradually decreased again, ending as softly as it began. In vocal music this effect is called *messa di voce*.

63. In music for stringed instruments of the violin family, the sign ⊓ indicates down-bow and the sign ∨ up-bow.

CHAPTER VI

EMBELLISHMENTS

64. *Embellishments* (*or graces*) (*Fr. agréments*) are ornamental tones, either represented in full in the score or indicated by certain signs. The following are the embellishments most commonly found: Trill (or shake), mordent, inverted mordent (or prall trill), turn (gruppetto), inverted turn, appoggiatura and acciaccatura.

Usage varies greatly in the interpretation of the signs representing these embellishments and it is impossible to give examples of all the different forms. The following definitions represent therefore only the most commonly found examples and the most generally accepted interpretations.

65. The *trill* (*or shake*) consists of the rapid alternation of two tones to the full value of the printed note. The lower of these two tones is represented by the printed note, while the upper one is the next higher tone in the diatonic scale of the key in which the composition is written. The interval between the two tones may therefore be either a half-step or a whole-step.

Whether the trill is to begin with the principal tone (represented by the printed note) or with the one above is a matter of some dispute among theorists and performers, but it may safely be said that the majority of modern writers on the subject would have it begin on the principal tone rather than on the tone above. Fig. 40.

When the principal note is preceded by a small note on the degree above, it is of course understood that the trill begins on the tone above. Fig. 41.

The trill is indicated by the sign *tr*~~~~~~~~~~~

Fig. 40.

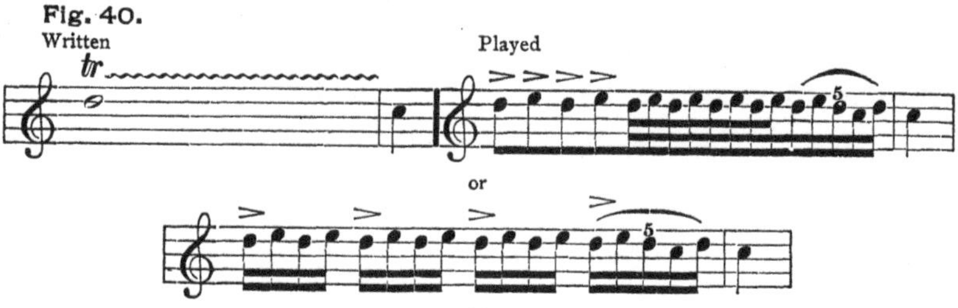

Fig. 41.

Written   Played

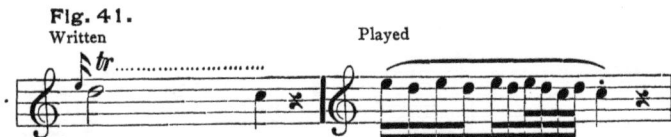

The above examples would be termed *perfect trills* because they close with a turn. By inference, an *imperfect trill* is one closing without a turn.

66. The *mordent* ᷈ consists of three tones; first the one represented by the printed note; second the one next below it in the diatonic scale; third the one represented by the printed note again.

Fig. 42.

Written Played Written Played

67. The *double (or long) mordent* has five tones (sometimes seven) instead of three, the first two of the three tones of the regular mordent being repeated once or more. (See Fig. 43.)

In the case of both mordent and double-mordent the tones are sounded as quickly as possible, the time taken by the embellishment being subtracted from the value of the principal note as printed.

Fig. 43.

Written   Played

68. The *inverted mordent* ᷉ (note the absence of the vertical line) is like the mordent except that the tone below is replaced by the tone above in each case. This ornament is sometimes called a "transient shake" because it is really only a part of the more elaborate grace called "trill." (See Fig. 44.)

Fig. 44.

Written Played

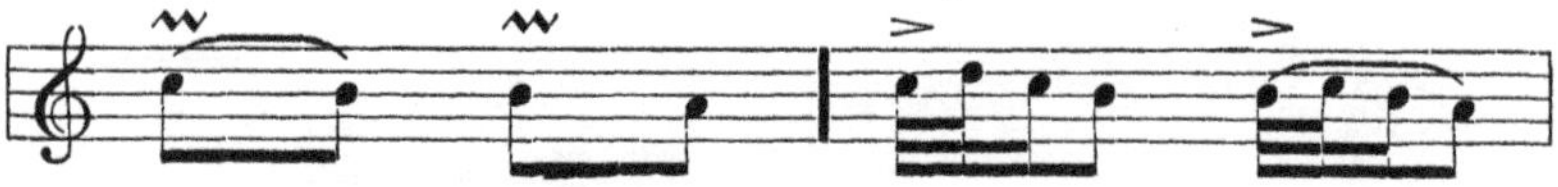

The confusion at present attending the interpretation of the last two embellishments described, might be largely obviated if the suggestion of a recent writer [1] to call the one the *upward mordent*, and the other the *downward mordent* were to be universally adopted.

69. The *turn* consists of four tones; first, the diatonic scale-tone above the principal tone; second, the principal tone itself; third, the tone below the principal tone; and fourth, the principal tone again.

When the sign (~ or ∾) occurs over a note of small value in rapid tempo (Fig. 45) the turn consists of four tones of equal value; but if it occurs over a note of greater value, or in a slow tempo, the tones are usually played quickly (like the mordent), and the fourth tone is then held until the time-value of the note has expired. (Fig. 46.)

Fig. 45.

(*a*) *Allegro*

Written Played

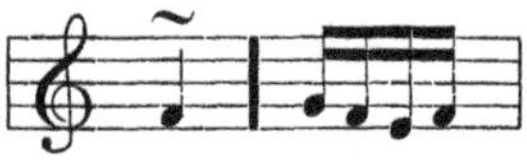

Fig. 46.

(*b*) *Adagio*

Written Played

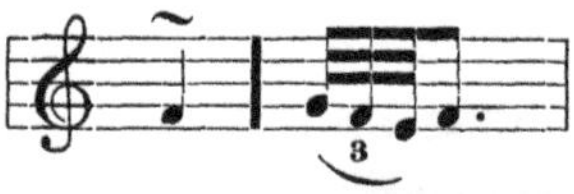

70. *When the turn-sign is placed a little to the right of the note* the principal tone is sounded first and held to almost its full time-value, then the turn is played just before the next tone of the melody. In this case the four tones are of equal length as in the first example. (See Fig. 47.)

Fig. 47.

Written Played

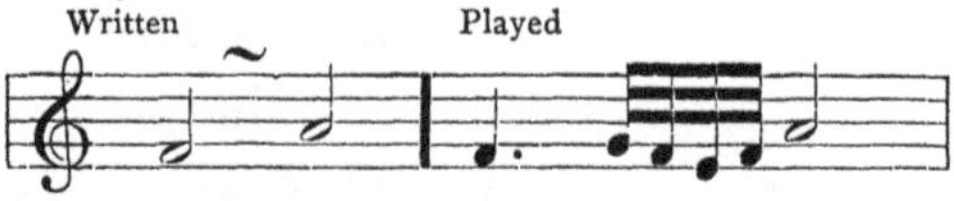

The student should note the difference between these two effects; in the case of a turn *over* the note the turn comes at the beginning, but in the case of the sign *after* the note the turn comes at the very end. But in both cases the time taken by the embel-

[1] Elson — Dictionary of Music, article *mordent.*

lishment is taken from the time-value of the principal note. For further details see Grove's Dictionary of Music and Musicians, Vol. V, p. 184. Also Elson, op. cit. p. 274.

71. Sometimes an accidental occurs with the turn, and in this case when written above the sign it refers to the highest tone of the turn, but when written below, to the lowest (Fig. 48).

Fig. 48.
Written   Played

72. In the *inverted turn* the order of tones is reversed, the lowest one coming first, the principal tone next, the highest tone third, and the principal tone again, last.

Fig. 49.
Written   Played
             Allegro   *Adagio*

73. The *appoggiatura* (lit. *leaning note*) consists of an ornamental tone introduced before a tone of a melody, thus delaying the melody tone until the ornamental tone has been heard. The time taken for this ornamental tone is taken from that of the melody tone.

The appoggiatura was formerly classified into *long appoggiatura* and *short appoggiatura*, but modern writers seem to consider the term "short appoggiatura" to be synonymous with acciaccatura[1], and to avoid confusion the word *acciaccatura* will be used in this sense, and defined under its own heading.

74. Three rules for the interpretation of the appoggiatura are commonly cited, viz.:

(1) When it is possible to divide the principal tone into halves, then the appoggiatura receives one-half the value of the printed note. (Fig. 50.)

[1] In organ music the acciaccatura is still taken to mean that the embellishing tone and the melody tone are to be sounded together, the former being then instantly released, while the latter is held to its full time-value.

(2) When the principal note is dotted (division into halves being therefore not possible), the appoggiatura receives two-thirds of the value. (Fig. 51.)

(3) When the principal note is tied to a note of smaller denomination the appoggiatura receives the value of the first of the two notes. (Fig. 52.)

Fig. 50.
Written   Played

Fig. 51.
Written   Played

Fig. 52.
Written   Played

75. The *acciaccatura* (or short appoggiatura) is written like the appoggiatura except that it has a light stroke across its stem. It has no definite duration-value, but is sounded as quickly as possible, taking its time from that of the principal tone. The appoggiatura is always accented, but the acciaccatura never is, the stress always falling on the melody tone. (See Grove, op. cit. Vol. I, p. 96.)

The use of embellishments is on the wane, and the student of to-day needs the above information only to aid him in the interpretation of music written in previous centuries. In the early days of instrumental music it was necessary to introduce graces of all sorts because the instruments in use were not capable of sustaining tone for any length of time; but with the advent of the modern piano with its comparatively great sustaining power, and also with the advent in vocal music of a new style of singing (German Lieder singing as contrasted with Italian coloratura singing), ornamental tones were used less and less, and when found now are usually written out in full in the score instead of being indicated by signs.

CHAPTER VII

SCALES

76. A *scale* (from *scala*, a Latin word meaning *ladder;* Ger. *Ton-leiter*) is an ascending or descending series of tones, progressing according to some definite system, and all bearing (in the case of tonality scales at least) a very intimate relation to the first tone — the *key-tone* or *tonic*. (See p. 28, Sec. 78; also note 1 at bottom of p. 38.)

Many different kinds of scales have existed in various musical eras, the point of resemblance among them all being the fact that they have all more or less recognized the *octave* as the natural limit of the series. The difference among the various scales has been in the selection of intervals between the scale-tones, and, consequently, in the number of tones within the octave. Thus̲ *e.g.*, in our major scale the intervals between the tones are all whole-steps except two (which are half-steps), and the result is a scale of *eight* tones (including in this number both the key-tone and its octave): but in the so-called *pentatonic* scale of the Chinese and other older civilizations we find larger intervals (*e.g.*, the step-and-a-half), and consequently a smaller number of tones within the octave. Thus in the scale upon which many of the older Scotch folk songs are based the intervals are arranged as follows:

1 whole step 2 whole step 3 step-and-a-half 4 whole step 5 step-and-a-half 6

The result is a scale of six tones, corresponding approximately with C—D—E—G—A—C in our modern system.

The term *pentatonic* is thus seen to be a misnomer since the sixth tone is necessary for the completion of the series, just as the eighth tone is essential in our diatonic scales.

The following Chinese tune (called "Jasmine") is based on the pentatonic scale.

77. In studying the theory of the scale the student should bear in mind the fact that a scale is not an arbitrary series of tones which some one has invented, and which others are required to make use of.   It is rather the result of accustoming the ear to certain melodic combinations (which were originally hit upon by accident), and finally analyzing and systematizing these combinations into a certain definite order or arrangement.   The application of this idea may be verified when it is recalled that most primitive peoples have invented melodies of some sort, but that only in modern times, and particularly since the development of instrumental music, have these melodies been analyzed, and the scale upon which they have been based, discovered, the inventors of the melodies being themselves wholly ignorant of the existence of such scales.

78. A *key* is a number of tones grouping themselves naturally (both melodically and harmonically) about a central tone — the key tone.   The word *tonality* is often used synonymously with *key* in this sense.

The difference between *key* and *scale* is therefore this, that while both *key* and *scale* employ the same tone material, by *key* we mean the material in general, without any particular order or arrangement in mind, while by *scale* we mean the same tones, but now arranged into a regular ascending or descending series.   It should be noted in this connection also that not all scales present an equally good opportunity of having their tones used as a basis for tonality or key-feeling: neither the chromatic nor the whole-step scale possess the necessary characteristics for being used as tonality scales in the same sense that our major and minor scales are so used.

79. There are *three general classes of scales* extant at the present time, viz.: (1) Diatonic; (2) Chromatic; (3) Whole-tone.[1]

80. The word *diatonic* means "through the tones" (*i.e.*, through the tones of the key), and is applied to both major and minor scales of our modern tonality system.   In general a diatonic scale may be defined as one which proceeds by half-steps and whole-steps.   There is, however, one exception to

---

[1] If strictly logical terminology is to be insisted upon the whole-tone scale should be called the "whole-step" scale.

this principle, viz., in the progression six to seven in the harmonic minor scale, which is of course a step-and-a-half. (See p. 33, Sec. 86.)

81. A *major diatonic scale* is one in which the intervals between the tones are arranged as follows:

| 1 | whole step | 2 | whole step | 3 | half step | 4 | whole step | 5 | whole step | 6 | whole step | 7 | half step | 8 |

In other words, a major diatonic scale is one in which the intervals between three and four, and between seven and eight are half-steps, all the others being whole-steps. A composition based on this scale is said to be written in the major mode, or in a major key. The major diatonic scale may begin on any one of the twelve pitches C, C♯ or D♭, D, D♯ or E♭, E, F, F♯ or G♭, G, G♯ or A♭, A, A♯ or B♭, B, but in each case it is the same scale because the intervals between its tones are the same. We have then one major scale only, but this scale may be written in many different positions, and may be sung or played beginning on any one of a number of different pitches.

82. It is interesting to note that the major scale consists of two identical series of four tones each; *i.e.*, the first four tones of the scale are separated from one another by exactly the same intervals and these intervals appear in exactly the same order as in the case of the last four tones of the scale. Fig. 53 will make this clear. The first four tones of any diatonic scale (major or minor) are often referred to as the *lower tetrachord*[1] and the upper four tones as the *upper tetrachord*.

Fig. 53.

---

[1] The word *tetrachord* means literally "four strings" and refers to the primitive instrument, the four strings of which were so tuned that the lowest and the highest tones produced were a perfect fourth apart. With the Greeks the tetrachord was the unit of analysis as the octave is with us to-day, and all Greek scales are capable of division into two tetrachords, the arrangement of the intervals between the tones in each tetrachord differentiating one scale from another, but the tetrachords themselves always consisting of groups of four tones, the highest being a perfect fourth above the lowest.

It is interesting further to note that the upper tetrachord of any *sharp* scale is always used without change as the lower tetrachord of the next major scale involving sharps, while the lower tetrachord of any *flat* scale is used as the upper tetrachord of the next flat scale.   See Figs. 54 and 55.

Fig. 54.

Upper Tetrachord from Scale of C   New Tetrachord to complete Scale of G

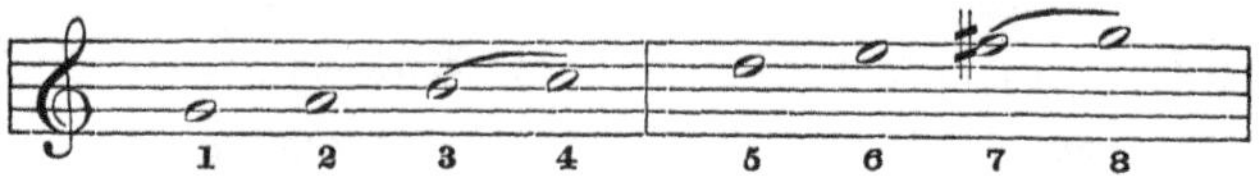

1   2   3   4   5   6   7   8

Fig. 55.

Lower Tetrachord from Scale of C   New Tetrachord to complete Scale of F

8   7   6   5   4   3   2   1

83. From the standpoint of staff notation the major scale may be written in fifteen different positions, as follows:

C, No sharps or flats   Signature and Key-note

G, One Sharp

D, Two Sharps

A, Three sharps

E, Four sharps

B, Five sharps

F♯, Six sharps

C♯, Seven sharps

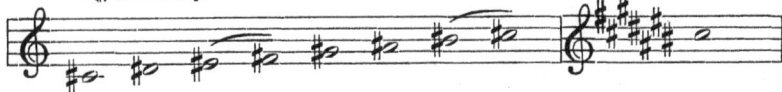

F, One Flat

B♭, Two Flats

E♭, Three Flats

A♭, Four Flats

D♭, Five Flats

G♭, Six Flats

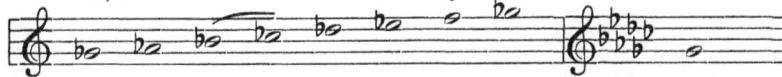

C♭, Seven Flats

It will be observed that in the above series of scales those beginning on F♯ and G♭ call for the same keys on the piano, *i.e.*, while the notation is different, the actual tones of the scale are the same. The scales of C♯ and D♭ likewise employ the same tones. When two scales thus employ the same tones but differ in notation they are said to be *enharmonic*. (cf. p. 38, Sec. 93.)

Note. — The student is advised to adopt some uniform method of writing scales, preferably the one followed in those given above, the necessary sharps and flats appearing before the notes in the scale and then repeated collectively at the end as a signature. He is also advised to repeat these scales and signatures over and over until absolute familiarity is attained. *E.g.*, E—F#—G#—A—B—C#—D#—E; signature, four sharps, F, C, G, and D.

CHAPTER VIII

SCALES (*Continued*)

84. The *minor diatonic scale* is used in several slightly different forms, but the characteristic interval between the first and third tones (which differentiates it from the major scale) remains the same in every case. This interval between the first and third tones consists of four half-steps in the major scale and of three half-steps in the minor scale and this difference in size has given rise to the designation *major* for the scale having the larger third, and *minor* for the scale having the smaller one.

85. *The original (or primitive) form* of the minor scale has its tones arranged as follows.

1 whole step   2 half step   3 whole step   4 whole step   5 half step   6 whole step   7 whole step   8

As its name implies, this is the oldest of the three forms (being derived from the old Greek Aeolian scale), but because of the absence of a "leading tone" it is suitable for the simplest one-part music only, and is therefore little used at present.

86. *The harmonic minor scale* is like the primitive form except that it substitutes a tone one half-step higher for the seventh tone of the older (*i.e.*, the primitive) form. This change was made because the development of writing music in several parts (particularly *harmonic* part-writing) made necessary a "leading tone," *i.e.*, a tone with a strong tendency to move on up to the key-tone as a closing point. In order

to secure a tone with such a strongly upward tendency the interval between *seven* and *eight* had to be reduced in size to a half-step.   It should be noted that this change in the seventh tone of the scale caused an interval of a step-and-a-half between the sixth and seventh tones of the scale.

| 1 | whole step | 2 | half step | 3 | whole step | 4 | whole step | 5 | half step | 6 | step and a half | 7 | half step | 8 |

87.   *The melodic minor scale* substitutes a tone one half-step higher than six as well as one a half-step higher than seven, but this change is made in the ascending scale only, the descending scale being like the primitive form.   The higher sixth (commonly referred to as the "raised sixth") was used to get rid of the unmelodic interval of a step-and-a-half[1] (augmented second), while the return to the primitive form in descending is made because the ascending form is too much like the tonic major scale.

| 1 | whole step | 2 | half step | 3 | whole step | 4 | whole step | 5 | whole step | 6 | whole step | 7 | half step | 8 | whole step |

| 7 | whole step | 6 | half step | 5 | whole step | 4 | whole step | 3 | half step | 2 | whole step | 1 |

This form is used only to a very limited extent, and then principally in vocal music, the harmonic form being in almost universal use in spite of the augmented second.

88.   The minor scale in its various positions (up to five sharps and five flats) and in all three forms follows: a composition based on any one of these forms (or upon a mixture of them, which often occurs) is said to be *in the minor mode.*   It will be noted that the first four tones are alike in all three forms; *i.e.*, the lower tetrachord in the minor scale is invariable no matter what may happen to the upper tetrachord.   The sign + marks the step-and-a-half.

---

[1] The step-and-a-half (augmented second) is "unmelodic" because it is the same size as a *minor third* and the mind finds it difficult to take in as a *second* (notes representing it being on adjacent staff-degrees) an interval of the same size as a third.

Primitive Form	Harmonic Form	Melodic Form	Signature

A Minor

E Minor

B Minor

F♯ Minor

C♯ Minor

G♯ Minor

D Minor

G Minor

C Minor

F Minor

B♭ Minor

Note. — The student is advised to recite the *harmonic form* of the minor scale as was suggested in the case of the major scale, noting that the "raised seventh" does not affect the key-signature. *E.g.,* — E—F♯—G—A—B—C—D♯—E; signature, one sharp, F.

89. A minor scale having the same signature as a major scale is said to be its *relative minor*. *E.g.*, — e is the relative minor of G, c of E♭, d of F, etc., the small letter being used to refer to the minor key or scale, while the capital letter indicates the major key or scale unless accompanied by the word *minor*. Relative keys are therefore defined as those having the same signature.   G and e are relative keys, as are also A and f♯, etc.

90. A minor scale beginning with the same tone as a major scale is referred to as its *tonic minor*. Thus, *e.g.*, c with three flats in its signature is the tonic minor of C with all degrees in natural condition; e with one sharp is the tonic minor of E with four sharps, etc.   Tonic keys are therefore those having the same key-tone.

91. The eight tones of the diatonic scale (both major and minor) are often referred to by specific names, as follows:

1. *Tonic* — the tone.   (This refers to the fact that the tonic is the principal tone, or generating tone of the key, *i.e.*, it is *the* tone.)

2. *Supertonic* — above the tone.

3. *Mediant* — midway between tonic and dominant.

4. *Sub-dominant* — the under dominant.   (This name does not refer to the position of the tone under the dominant but to the fact that the fifth below the tonic is also a dominant tone — the under dominant — just as the fifth above is the upper dominant).

5. *Dominant* — the governing tone.   (From the Latin word *dominus* meaning *master*.)

6. *Super-dominant* — above the dominant.
   or *Sub-mediant* — midway between tonic and sub-dominant.

7. *Leading tone* — the tone which demands resolution to the tonic (one-half step above it).

8. *Octave* — the eighth tone.

92. The syllables commonly applied to the various major and minor scales in teaching sight-singing are as follows:[1]

Major — DO, RE, MI, FA, SOL, LA, TI, DO.

Minor[2] — original — LA, TI, DO, RE, MI, FA, SOL, LA.

harmonic — LA, TI, DO, RE, MI, FA, SI, LA.

melodic — LA, TI, DO, RE, MI, FI, SI, LA, SOL, FA, MI, RE, DO, TI, LA.

It is interesting to study the changes in both spelling and pronunciation that have occurred (and are still occurring) in these syllables. The first one (ut) was changed to *DO* as early as the sixteenth century because of the difficulty of producing a good singing tone on *ut*. For the same reason and also in order to avoid having two diatonic syllables with the same initial letter, the tonic-sol-fa system (invented in England about 1812 and systematized about 1850) changed SI to TI and this change has been almost universally adopted by teachers of sight-singing in this country. The more elaborate tonic-sol-fa spelling of the diatonic syllables (DOH, LAH, etc.), has not, however, been favorably received in this country and the tendency seems to be toward still further simplification rather than toward elaboration. It is probable that further changes in both spelling and pronunciation will be made in the near future, one such change that seems especially desirable being some other syllable than RE for the second tone of the major scale, so that the present syllable may be reserved for "flat-two," thus providing a uniform vowel-sound for all intermediate tones of the descending chromatic scale, as is already the case in the ascending form.

---

[1] These syllables are said to have been derived originally from the initial syllables of the "Hymn to Saint John," the music of which was a typical Gregorian chant. The application of these syllables to the scale tones will be made clear by reference to this hymn as given below. It will be observed that this hymn provided syllables only for the six tones of the *hexachord* then recognized; when the octave scale was adopted (early in the sixteenth century) the initial letters of the last line (s and i) were combined into a syllable for the seventh tone.

Ut que-ant lax - is   *Re* - so - na - re   fi - bris *Mi* -   ra   ges - to-rum

Fa - mu - li   tu -   o - rum   *Sol* -   ve   pol - lu - ti   *La* - bi - i   re - a - tum

Sanc - te   Jo - han - nes.

[2] A considerable number of teachers (particularly those who did not learn to sing by syllable in childhood) object to calling the tonic of the minor scale *la*, insisting that both major and minor tonic should be called *do*. According to this plan the syllables used in singing the harmonic minor scale would be: DO, RE, ME, FA, SOL, LE, TI, DO.
There is no particular basis for this theory, for although all scales must of course begin with the key-tone or tonic, this tonic may be referred to by any syllable which will serve as a basis for an association process enabling one to feel the force of the tone as a closing point — a *home tone*. Thus in the Dorian mode the tonic would be RE, in the Phrygian, MI, etc.

93. The *chromatic scale*[1] is one which proceeds always by half-steps. Its intervals are therefore always equal no matter with what tone it begins. Since, however, we have (from the standpoint of the piano keyboard) five pairs of tones[2] which are enharmonically the same, it may readily be seen that the chromatic scale might be notated in all sorts of fashions, and this is in fact the real status of the matter, there being no one method uniformly agreed upon by composers.

Parry (Grove's Dictionary, article *chromatic*) recommends writing the scale with such accidentals as can occur in chromatic chords without changing the key in which the passage occurs. Thus ,taking C as a type, " the first accidental will be Db, as the upper note of the minor ninth on the tonic; the next will be Eb, the minor third of the key; the next F♯, the major third of the supertonic — all of which can occur without causing modulation — and the remaining two will be Ab and Bb, the minor sixth and seventh of the key." According to this plan the chromatic scale beginning with C would be spelled — C, Db, D, Eb, E, F, F♯, G, Ab, A, Bb, B, C — the form being the same both ascending and descending. This is of course written exclusively from a harmonic standpoint and the advantage of such a form is its definiteness.

94. For *sight-singing purposes* the chromatic scale[3] is usually written by representing the intermediate tones in ascending by sharps, (in some cases naturals and double-sharps), and the intermediate tones in descending by flats (sometimes naturals and double-flats). The chromatic scale in nine different positions, written from this standpoint, follows, and the syllables most commonly applied in sight-singing have also been added. In the first two scales the student of harmony is asked to note that because of the very common prac-

---

[1] The student should differentiate between the so-called "tonality" scales like the major and minor, the tones of which are actually used as a basis for "key-feeling" with the familiar experience of coming home to the tonic after a melodic or harmonic excursion, and on the other hand the purely artificial and mechanical construction of the chromatic scale.

[2] Many other enharmonic notations are possible, altho the "five pairs of tones" above referred to are the most common. Thus E♯ and F are enharmonically the same, as are also Cb and B, C♯ and B✕, etc.

[3] The word *chromatic* means literally *colored* and was first applied to the intermediate tones because by using them the singer could get smoother and more diversely-shaded progressions, *i.e.*, could get more *color* than by using only the diatonic tones. Composers were not long discovering the peculiar value of these additional tones and soon found that these same tones were exceedingly valuable also in modulating, hence the two uses of intermediate tones at the present time,— first, to embellish a melody; second, to modulate to another key.

tice of modulating to the dominant and sub-dominant keys, the intermediate tones ♯4 and ♭7 are quite universally used in both ascending and descending melody passages. In other words the scales that follow would more nearly represent actual usage if in each case ♯4 (FI) were substituted for ♭5 (SE) in the descending scale; and if ♭7 (TE) were substituted for ♯6 (LI) in the ascending form.

C

DO di RE ri MI FA fi SOL si LA li TI DO

TI te LA le SOL se FA MI me RE ra Do

G

DO di RE ri Mi FA fi SOL si LA li TI DO

TI te LA le SOL se FA MI me RE ra DO

D

A

E

F

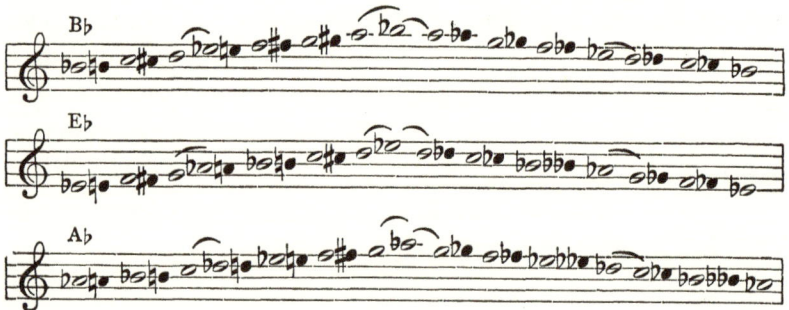

Note. — In writing chromatic scales from this sight-singing standpoint the student is urged to adopt a three-step process; first, writing the major diatonic scale both ascending and descending; second, marking the half-steps; third, inserting accidental notes calling for the intermediate tones. In the above chromatic scales these intermediate tones have been represented by black note-heads so as to differentiate them from the notes representing diatonic scale tones.

95. The *whole-step scale* (the third type mentioned in Sec. 79) is, as its name implies, a scale in which the intervals between the tones consist in every instance of whole-steps. This reduces the number of tones in the scale to seven. Beginning with C the scale reads: C, D, E, F♯ or G♭, A♭, B♭, C. This scale has been used somewhat extensively by the ultra-modern French school of composition represented by Debussy, Ravel, and others, but is not making any progress toward universal adoption. The remarks of a recent English writer[1] on this subject may be interesting to the student who is puzzled by the apparant present-day tendencies of French music. He says:

" The student of some interesting modern developments will also speedily discover that the adoption of the so-called whole-tone scale as a basis of music is, except upon a keyed instrument tuned to the compromise of equal temperament, unnatural and impossible. No player upon a stringed instrument can play the scale of whole-tones and arrive at an octave which is in tune with the starting note, unless he deliberately changes one of the notes on the road and alters it while playing it. The obvious result of the application of the whole-tone scale to an orchestra or a string quartet would be to force them to adopt the equal temperament of the pianoforte, and play every interval except the octave out of tune. When this modification had taken hold all music in the pure scale would be distorted and destroyed, unless string players were to face the

[1] Stanford — Musical Composition (1911) p. 17.

practically impossible drudgery of studying both the equal temperament and the pure scale from the start, and were able to tackle either form at a moment's notice. A thorough knowledge of the natural genesis of the scale of western nations will be the best antidote to fads founded upon ignorance of it. It is a curious commentary upon this question that Wagner, in the opening of the third act of *Tristan* (bars 6 to 10), experimented with the whole-tone scale and drew his pen through it, as was to be expected from a composer whose every work proves the writer to have had the pure scale inbred in him."

There may be some difference of opinion among acousticians as to whether Mr. Stanford is correct in his scientific assumptions regarding the difference between "tempered" and "pure" scales,[1] but even so, there is a far more potent reason why the whole-step scale will probably never become popular as the major and minor scales now are, viz., the fact that it offers no possibility of *inculcating tonality feeling*, which has always been the basis of even the simplest primitive music. Tonality scales give rise to a feeling of alternate periods of contraction and relaxation — an active tone (or chord) followed by a passive one, but no such effect is possible in the whole-step scale, and it seems suitable therefore only for that class of music whose outlines are *purposely intended to be* vague and indefinite — the impressionistic style of music writing.

---

[1] Recent tests in Germany seem to prove conclusively that the *tempered* scale is the scale ordinarily employed by both vocalists and players on stringed instruments, and that the ideal of and agitation for a *pure* (i. e., *untempered*) scale in vocal and in string music is somewhat of a myth.

CHAPTER IX

AUXILIARY WORDS AND ENDINGS

96. Being a list of articles, adverbs, conjunctions, prepositions, and endings, often utilized in compounding terms relating to musical effects.

A — preposition — variously translated to, at, for, by, in, with, towards.
   A cappella — in church style.
   A capriccio — at the fancy of the performer.
   A deux mains — for two hands.
   A mezza voce — with half voice.
A la, or *alla* — in the manner of.   *Alla marcia* — in the style of a march.
Assai — very, or very much.   *Allegro assai* — very fast.
Ben — well.   *Ben marcato* — well marked.
Coi, con, col, colla, colle, collo — with, or with the.
   Con amore — with tenderness.
   Colla voce — with the voice.
Come — as, like.   *Come primo* — as at first.
Contra — against.   In compound words means "an octave below."
Da — from.   *Da Capo* — from the head.
Di — by, with, of, for.   *Di bravura* — with daring.
Di molto — exceedingly — very much.   *Allegro di molto* — exceedingly rapid.
Doppio — double.   *Doppio movimento* — double movement.
E, ed, et — and.   *Cresc. et accel.* — louder and faster.
Ensemble — together, the opposite of solo.
Il, La, l', le — the.   *Il basso* — the bass.   *L'istesso tempo* — the same speed.
Il piu — the most.   *Il piu forte possible* — as loudly as possible.
Issimo — Italian superlative ending.   *Forte — fortissimo.*
Ino, etto — Italian diminutive endings.   *Andante — andantino.   Poco — pochetto.*
Meno — less.   *Meno forte* — less loud.
Mente — the ending which changes a noun or adjective to an adverb.   *Largo largamente.*
Mezzo or *mezza* — half, or medium.   *Mezzo forte* — medium loud.
Molto — much, or very much.   *Molto cresc.* — very much louder.
Nel, nella, etc. — in the, or at the.   *Nel battere* — at the down beat.
Non — not.   *Non tanto* — not too much.
Ossia — or else.   *Ossia piu facile* — or else more easily.
Per — for.   *Per il violino* — for the violin.
Peu — little.   *Un peu cresc.* — a little increase in tone.
Più — more.   *Più forte* — more loudly.

42

Poco — little. *Poco a poco* — little by little.

Poi — then. *E poi la coda* — and then the coda.

Possibile — possible. *Forte possibile* — as loudly as possible.

Quasi — in the manner of. *Allegro quasi andante* — a fairly rapid movement, yet in the style of an andante; almost as slow as an andante.

Sans — without. *Sans pedales* — without pedals.

Sempre — always, or continually. *Sempre forte* — a long passage to be played forte throughout its entirety.

Senza — without. *Senza accompagnamento* — without accompaniment.

Sino, sin — as far as. See p. 14, note.

Solo — alone. Opposite of ensemble.

Sub — under or lower. *Subdominant* — the under dominant.

Tanto — same as *troppo*, q. v.

Tre — three. *Tre corde* — three strings.

Très — very. *Très vivement* — very lively.

Troppo — too much. *Non tanto allegro*, or *non troppo allegro* — not too fast.

Una, un, uno — one, or *a*. *Una corda* — one string. *Un peu* — a little.

A working knowledge of these auxiliary terms will aid the student greatly in arriving at the meaning of hundreds of terms without stopping to look up each individual one.

CHAPTER X

MEASURE

97. From the standpoint of the eye, a *measure* is that portion of the staff found between two bars, (in certain cases this space may be less than a measure, as *e.g.*, at the beginning and end of a movement); but from the standpoint of the ear a single, isolated measure is not possible, and the term must therefore be defined in the plural form.

Measures are similarly accented groups of evenly-spaced beats, each group having at least one accented and one non-accented beat. The strongest accent falls normally on the first beat in the measure.

Two essential characteristics are involved in the ordinary musical measure:

(1) A group of even beats (or pulses), always felt, though not always actually sounded, one or more of these beats being stronger than the rest;

(2) Certain rhythmic figures (♫, ♫♪, ♩.♪, ♫♫, etc.) which form the actual musical content of these groups.

The student will note the essential difference between rhythm and measure. Rhythm is the regular recurrence of accent in a series of beats (or pulses), while measure is the grouping of these beats according to some specified system. In listening to a piece of music, two hearers A and B may feel the *rhythm* equally strongly, but A may subjectively group the beats into — *one*, two | *one*, two | — etc., while B feels the groups as — *one*, two, *three*, four | *one*, two, *three*, four | — etc. Rhythm is thus seen to be a fundamental thing, inherent in the music itself, while measure is to a certain extent at least an arbitrary grouping which musicians have adopted for practical purposes.

98. In *syncopation* the normal system of accenting is temporarily suspended and the accented tone falls on the regularly unaccented part of the measure. Syncopation may therefore be defined as the temporary interruption of a normal

44

series of accents, *i.e.*, accenting a beat that is usually not accented. Thus *e.g.*, in Fig. 56, measure *one* has the regular
system of accents normally found in four-quarter-measure,
(strong accent on one, secondary accent on three); but measure *three* has only one accent, and it falls on the second beat.

Fig. 56.

99. Measures are usually classified as *simple* and *compound*.
A *simple measure* is one which has but a single accent, *i.e.*,
the measure cannot be divided into smaller constituent groups.
There are two main classes of simple measures, two-beat
measure, and three-beat measure. A *compound measure* is (as
its name implies) one made up by combining two or more
simple measures, or by the elaboration of a single measure
(in slow tempo) into several constituent groups. The principal compound measures are four-beat and six-beat, both
being referred to as compound-duple measures. Five-beat,
seven-beat, nine-beat, and twelve-beat measures are also
classified as compound measures.

An English writer[1] classifies measures as duple, triple, or quadruple, specifying that
a simple measure is one in which each beat is represented by a note whose value can be
divided into halves (♩ = ♪ ♪, 𝅗𝅥 = ♩ ♩ etc.) and that a compound measure
is one in which each beat is represented by a dotted-note, whose value can be divided
into three parts, (♩. = ♪ ♪ ♪, 𝅗𝅥. = ♩ ♩ ♩). There is thus seen to be
considerable difference of opinion as to the meaning of the words *simple* and *compound*
when applied in this connection, the principal question at issue being whether four-
beat measure is an individual variety, or whether it is a variety compounded out of
two-beat measures, either by placing two of these in a group or by the elaboration of a
single measure into a larger number of beats, as is often necessary in slow tempi. Perhaps the easiest way out of the difficulty is to admit that both may be true — but in different compositions. That is, it is frequently impossible to tell whether a composition
that is being listened to is in two-beat, or in four-beat measure; and yet it *is* sometimes possible so to discriminate. Since, however, one cannot in the majority of cases
distinguish between two-beat and four-beat measures, it will probably be best to leave
the original classification intact and regard four-beat measure as a compound variety.

---

[1] Pearse — Rudiments of Musical Knowledge, p. 37.

100. The *commonest varieties of measure* are:

    1. *Duple* (sometimes called even measure, or even time), in which there are two beats, the first one being accented. Examples of duple measure are $\frac{2}{4}$, $\frac{2}{8}$, $\frac{2}{2}$, two-quarter,[1] two-eighth, and two-half measure, respectively.

    2. *Triple*, (the old perfect measure), in which there are three beats, the first one being accented, the second and third unaccented. Examples are $\frac{3}{8}$, $\frac{3}{4}$, $\frac{3}{2}$, three-eighth, three-quarter, and three-half measure, respectively.

    3. *Quadruple*, in which there are four beats, the first and third being accented (primary accent on *one*, secondary accent on *three*), the second and fourth unaccented. (See note above, under Sec. 99.)

    4. *Sextuple*, in which there are six beats, the first and fourth being accented, the others not. In rapid tempi this is always taken as compound duple measure, a dotted quarter note having a beat. It will be noted that the two measures $\frac{6}{8}$ ♪♪♪ ♪♪♪ | ♩· ♩· | are identical in effect with $\frac{2}{4}$ ♪♪♪ ♪♪♪ | ♩ ♩ |.

101. Other varieties of measure sometimes found are $\frac{9}{8}$ and $\frac{12}{8}$, but these are practically always taken as three-beat and four-beat measures respectively, being equivalent to these if each group of three tones is thought of as a triplet.

$\frac{9}{8}$ ♪♪♪ ♪♪♪ ♩. is identical in effect with $\frac{3}{4}$ ♪♪♪ ♪♪♪ ♩

102. *Quintuple* (five-beat) and *septuple* (seven-beat) measures are occasionally met with, but these are rare and will always be sporadic. The five-beat measure is taken as a combination of three and two, or of two and three (sometimes a mixture of both in the same composition), while the

---

[1] For explanation of terminology, see p. 48, Sec. 106.

seven-beat measure is taken in groups of four and three, or of three and four.

103. The sign ₵ is usually understood to mean four-quarter measure, and the sign ₵, two-half measure, but usage varies somewhat, and the second sign is sometimes used to indicate four-half measure. It may safely be said however that the sign ₵ always indicates that a half-note has a beat. ₵ ₵ may occasionally be found indicating four-half measure but this is rare.

The student will note that the sign ₵ is not a *letter* C, but an incomplete circle, differentiating two-beat (imperfect) measure from three-beat (perfect) measure. See Appendix A, p. 106.

CHAPTER XI

TEMPO

104. The word *time* in musical nomenclature has been greatly abused, having been used to indicate:

(1) Rhythm; as "the time was wrong."

(2) Variety of measure-signature; as "two-four time."

(3) Rate of speed; as "the time was too slow."

To obviate the confusion naturally resulting from this three-fold and inexact use of the word, many teachers of music are adopting certain *changes in terminology* as noted in Sections 105, 106, and 107. Such changes may cause some confusion at first, but seem to be necessary if our musical terminology is to be at all exact.

105. The *first of the changes* mentioned in the above paragraph is to substitute the word *rhythm* for the word *time* when correcting mistakes involving misplaced accent, etc. *E.g.*, "Your *rhythm* in the third measure of the lower score was wrong," instead of "Your *time* — was wrong."

106. The *second change* mentioned would eliminate such blind and misleading expressions as "two-four time," "three-four time," "four-four time," "six-eight time," etc., and substitute therefor such self-explanatory designations as "two-quarter measure," "three-quarter measure," "four-quarter measure," "six-eighth measure," etc. *E.g.*, "The first movement of the Beethoven Sonata Op. 2, No. 3, is in *four-quarter measure*."

107. The *third change* referred to above would substitute the word *tempo* (plural — *tempi*) for the word *time* in all allusions to rate of speed. *E.g.*, "The scherzo was played in very rapid *tempo*."

The word *tempo* has been used in this connection so long by professional musicians that there can be no possible objection to it on the ground of its being a foreign word. In fact there is a decided advantage in having a word that is understood in all countries where modern music (*i.e.*, civilized music) is performed, and just here is found the principal reason for the popularity of the Italian language in musical terminology. Schumann, MacDowell and other well known composers have tried to break down this popularity by using their own respective vernaculars in both tempo and dynamic indications, but in spite of these attempts the Italian language is still quite universally used for this purpose, and deservedly so, for if we are to have a *music notation* that is universal, so that an American is able to play music written by a Frenchman or a German, or a Russian, then we ought also to have a certain number of expressions referring to tempo, etc., which will be understood by all, *i.e.*, a music terminology that is universal. The Italian language was the first in the field, is the most universally known in this particular at the present time, and is entirely adequate. It should therefore be retained in use as a sort of musical Esperanto.

108. There are several *ways of finding the correct tempo* of a composition:

1. From the metronomic indication found at the beginning of many compositions. Thus *e.g.*, the mark M.M. 92 (Maelzel's Metronome 92) means that if the metronome (either Maelzel's or some other reliable make) is set with the sliding weight at the figure 92 there will be 92 clicks per minute, and they will serve to indicate to the player or singer the rate at which the beats (or pulses) should follow one another. This is undoubtedly the most accurate means of determining tempi in spite of slight inaccuracies in metronomes[1] and of the mistakes which composers themselves often make in giving metronomic indications.

2. Another means of determining the tempo of a composition is to play it at different tempi and then to choose the one that "feels right" for that particular piece of music. This is perhaps the best means of getting at the correct tempo but is open only to the

---

[1] To test the accuracy of a metronome, set the weight at 60 and see if it beats seconds. If it gives more than 62 or 63 or less than 57 or 58 clicks per minute it will not be of much service in giving correct tempi and should be taken to a jeweller to be regulated.

musician of long experience, sure judgment, and sound scholarship.

3. A third method of finding tempi is through the interpretation of certain words used quite universally by composers to indicate the approximate rate of speed and the general mood of compositions. The difficulty with this method is that one can hardly find two composers who employ the same word to indicate the same tempo, so that no absolute rate of speed can be indicated, and in the last analysis the conductor or performer must fall back on the second method cited above — *i.e.*, individual judgment.

109. In spite of the inexactness of use in the case of expressions relating to tempo, these expressions are nevertheless extremely useful in giving at least a hint of what was in the composer's mind as he conceived the music that we are trying to interpret. Since a number of the terms overlap in meaning, and since the meaning of no single term is absolute, these expressions relating to tempo are best studied in groups. Perhaps the most convenient grouping is as follows:

1. *Grave* (lit. weighty, serious), *larghissimo, adagissimo,* and *lentissimo* — indicating the very slowest tempo used in rendering music.

2. *Largo,*[1] *adagio,*[2] and *lento* — indicating quite a slow tempo.

3. *Larghetto* (*i.e., a little largo*) and *adagietto* (*a little adagio*) — a slow tempo, but not quite so slow as *largo,* etc.

4. *Andante* (going, or walking, as contrasted with running) and *andantino* — indicating a moderately slow tempo.

---

[1] Largo, larghetto, etc., are derivatives of the Latin word *largus,* meaning large, broad.

[2] Adagio means literally at ease.

Andantino is now quite universally taken slightly faster than *andante*, in spite of the fact that if *andante* means "going," and if "*ino*" is the diminutive ending, then *andantino* means "going less," *i.e.*, more slowly!

5. *Moderato* — a moderate tempo.

6. *Allegro* and *allegretto*[1] — a moderately quick tempo, *allegretto* being usually interpreted as meaning a tempo somewhat slower than *allegro*.

The word *allegro* means literally happy, joyous, and this literal meaning is still *sometimes* applicable, but in the majority of instances the term refers only to rate of speed.

7. *Vivo, vivace,* (lit. lively) — a tempo between *allegro* and *presto*.

8. *Presto, prestissimo, vivacissimo,* and *prestissimo possibile* — the most rapid tempo possible.

---

[1] There has been some difference of opinion as to which of these two terms indicates the more rapid tempo: an analysis tells us that if *allegro* means quick, and if *etto* is the diminutive ending, then *allegretto* means a little quick — *i.e.*, slower than *allegro*. These two terms are, however, so closely allied in meaning that a dispute over the matter is a mere waste of breath.

CHAPTER XII

TEMPO *(Continued)*

110. Innumerable combinations of the words defined in Sec. 109 with one another and with other words occur. Some of these combinations with their approximate meanings follow. The meaning of any such expression not found in the list may usually be arrived at by consulting the terms defined in paragraph 109 and recalling the use of certain auxiliary terms quoted in Chapter IX.

Largo assai — very slow.

Largo di molto — very slow.

Largo ma non troppo — slow, but not too slow.

Largo un poco — slow, but not so slow as *largo*. (*Cf. larghetto.*)

Lentemente — slowly.

Lentando — with increasing slowness.

Très lentement — very slowly.

Lentissimente — very slowly.

Lentissimamente — very slowly.

Lento assai — very slowly.

Lento a capriccio — slowly but capriciously.

Lento di molto — very slowly.

Andante affetuoso — moderately slow, and with tenderness and pathos.

Andante amabile — moderately slow, and lovingly.

Andante cantabile — moderately slow, and in singing style.

Andante grazioso — moderately slow, and gracefully.

Andante maestoso — moderately slow, and majestically.

Andante con moto — slightly faster than *andante*.

Andante (ma) non troppo — not too slowly.

Andante pastorale — moderately slow, and in simple and unaffected style; (*lit.* rural, pastoral).

Andante quasi allegro — almost as rapid in tempo as *allegro;* (lit. an *andante* in the style of *allegro*).

Andante sostenuto — moderately slow and sustained.

Allegrissimo — much faster than *allegro*. (The superlative degree of *allegro*.)

Allegro agitato — a moderately rapid tempo, and in agitated style.

Allegro appassionato — a moderately rapid tempo, and in passionate style.

Allegro assai (very *allegro*) — faster than *allegro*.

Allegro commodo — a conveniently rapid tempo.

Allegro con brio — an *allegro* played in brilliant style. Faster than *allegro*

Allegro con fuoco — an *allegro* played with fire, *i.e.*, with extreme animation. Faster than *allegro*.

Allegro con spirito — an *allegro* performed with spirit.

Allegro con moto — faster than *allegro*.

Allegro di bravura — an *allegro* performed in brilliant style, *i.e.*, demanding great skill in execution.

Allegro furioso (furiously) — quicker than *allegro;* very brilliant.

Allegro giusto — an *allegro* movement, but in exact rhythm.

Allegro ma grazioso — an *allegro* played in graceful style.

Allegro (ma) non tanto — an *allegro* movement, but not too rapid.

Allegro (ma) non troppo — an *allegro* movement, but not too rapid.

Allegro (ma) non presto — an *allegro* movement, but not too rapid.

Allegro moderato — slower than *allegro*.

Allegro vivace — faster than *allegro*.

Presto assai — as rapidly as possible.

Presto (ma) non troppo — a *presto* movement, but not too rapid.

III. There are certain *terms which indicate a modification of the normal tempo* of a movement, these being divided into two classes, (*a*) those terms which indicate in general a slower tempo, and (*b*) those which indicate in general a more rapid tempo. The further subdivisions of these two classes are shown below.

(*a*) Terms indicating a slower tempo.

    1. Terms indicating a *gradual* retard.

       Ritenente, (rit.), ritenuto (rit.), ritardando (rit.), rallentando (rall.), slentando.

    2. Terms indicating a tempo which is to become definitely slower *at once.*

       Più lento (lit. more slowly), *meno mosso* (lit. less movement).

    3. Terms indicating a slower tempo combined with an increase in power.

       Largando, allargando. These words are both derived from *largo*, meaning large, broad.

(For terms indicating both slower tempo and softer tone, see page 59, Sec. 127.)

The student should note the difference between groups 1 and 2 as given above: the terms in group 1 indicate that each measure, and even each pulse in the measure, is a little slower than the preceding one, while such terms as *piu lento* and *meno mosso* indicate a rate of speed becoming instantly slower and extending over an entire phrase or passage. Some composers (*e.g.*, Beethoven and Couperin) have evidently had this same distinction in mind between *rallentando* and *ritardando* on the one hand, and *ritenuto* and *ritenente* on the other, considering the former (*rall.* and *rit.*) to indicate a gradually slackening speed, and the latter (*ritenuto* and *ritenente*) to indicate a definitely slower rate. The majority of composers do not however differentiate between them in this way, and it will therefore hardly be worth while for the student to try to remember the distinction.

(*b*) Terms indicating a more rapid tempo.

1. Terms indicating a gradual acceleration.

Accelerando, affrettando (this term implies some degree of excitement also), *stringendo, poco a poco animato.*

2. Terms indicating a tempo which is to become definitely faster at once.

Più allegro, più tosto, più mosso, stretto, un poco animato.

112. After any modification in tempo (either faster or slower) has been suggested it is usual to indicate a return to the normal rate by some such expression as *a tempo* (lit. in time), *a tempo primo* (lit. in the first time), *tempo primo*, or *tempo.*

113. *Tempo rubato* (or *a tempo rubato*) means literally *in robbed time, i.e.*, duration taken from one measure or beat and given to another, but in modern practice the term is quite generally applied to any irregularity of rhythm or tempo not definitely indicated in the score.

The terms *ad libitum*, (*ad lib.*), *a piacere*, and *a capriccio*, also indicate a modification of the tempo at the will of the performer. *Ad libitum* means at liberty; *a piacere*, at pleasure; and *a capriccio*, at the caprice (of the performer).

114. The term *tempo giusto* is the opposite of *tempo rubato* (and of the other terms defined in paragraph 113). It means literally *in exact time*. (*Tempo giusto* is sometimes translated *quite rapidly*,[1] but this is very unusual.)

---

[1] Bussler — Elements of Notation and Harmony, p. 76.

115. *L'istesso tempo* means — at the same rate of speed. *E.g.*, when a measure signature changes from $\frac{2}{4}$ to $\frac{6}{8}$ with a change in beat-note from a quarter to a dotted-quarter, but with the same tempo carried through the entire movement.

116. *Tenuto* (*ten.*) indicates that a tone or chord is to be held to its full value. This word is sometimes used after a staccato passage to show that the staccato effect is to be discontinued, but is often used merely as a warning not to slight a melody-tone — *i.e.*, to give it its full value.

117. *Veloce* means — swiftly, and is applied to brilliant passages (*e.g.*, cadenzas) which are to be played as rapidly as possible without much regard for measure rhythm. The words *rapidamente*, *brillante* and *volante* (flying) have the same meaning as *veloce*.

118. The following *expressions referring to tempo* are also in common use but cannot easily be classified with any of the groups already defined.

Con moto — with motion; *i.e.*, not too slow.
Pesante — slowly, heavily.
Doppio movimento — twice as rapid as before.
Tempo ordinario — in ordinary tempo.
Tempo comodo — in convenient tempo.
Sempre lento malinconico assai — always slowly and in a very melancholy style.
Animando, animato, con anima — with animation.
Agitato — agitated.

119. *Tempo di marcia* is given by Riemann (Dictionary of Music, p. 783) as equivalent to *andante*, M.M. 72 — 84. The same writer gives *tempo di menuetto* as equivalent to *allegretto*, and *tempo di valso* as equivalent to *allegro moderato* (which he regards as indicating a more rapid tempo than *allegretto*).

CHAPTER XIII

DYNAMICS

120. The word *dynamics* (cf. dynamic — the opposite of static) as used in the nomenclature of music has to do with the various degrees of power (*i.e.*, the comparative loudness and softness) of tones.

As in the case of words referring to tempo, the expressions referring to *dynamics* are always relative, never absolute; it is possible to indicate that one measure is to be louder than another, but it is not possible (nor desirable) to indicate exactly how loud either is to be. Thus *dynamics*, perhaps even more than tempo, will be seen to depend on the taste of the performer or conductor.

The following *words referring to dynamics* are in common use:

Pianisissimo (ppp) — as softly as possible. (It will be noted that this is a sort of hyper-superlative of *piano*.)
Pianissimo (pp) — very softly. (The superlative of *piano*.)
Piano (p) — softly.
Mezzo piano (mp) — medium softly.
Mezzo forte (mf) — medium loudly.
Forte (f) — loudly (lit. strong).
Fortissimo (ff) — very loudly. (The superlative of *forte*.)
Fortisissimo (fff) — as loudly as possible.
The lack of a one-word comparative degree in the case of both *piano* and *forte* seems to necessitate the hyper-superlative degree as given above, but the practice of using four, or even five *p*'s or *f*'s is not desirable.

121. The terms defined in Sec. 120 are often combined with others, as *e.g.*,

Pianissimo possibile — as softly as possible.
Piano assai — very softly.
Fortissimo possibile — as loudly as possible.
Forte piano (fp) — loud, followed at once by soft.

As in the case of terms relating to tempo, the meaning of many other expressions relating to *dynamics* may easily be arrived at by recalling the list of auxiliary terms quoted under Sec. 96.

122. The terms *sforzando, forzando, sforzato* and *forzato* all indicate a strong accent on a single tone or chord. These words are abbreviated as follows: — *sf, fz,* and *sfz,* the abbreviation being placed directly above (sometimes below) the note or chord affected. The signs ∧ and ➤ are also commonly used to indicate such an accent.

In interpreting these accent marks the student must bear in mind again the fact that they have a relative rather than an absolute meaning: the mark *sf* occurring in the midst of a *piano* passage will indicate a much milder form of accent than would the same mark occurring in the midst of a *forte* passage.

123. The words *rinforzando* and *rinforzato* (abb. — *rinf.* and *rfz.*) mean literally *reinforced,* and are used to indicate a sudden increase in power usually extending over an entire phrase or passage instead of applying only to a single tone or chord as in the case of *sforzando,* etc.

124. *Crescendo* (abb. — *cresc.* or ◁⎯⎯) means a gradual increase in power. It will be noted that this word does not mean *loud,* nor does it mean a sudden increase in power unless accompanied by some auxiliary term such as *subito,* or *molto.*

Broadly speaking there are *two varieties of crescendo:* (1) that in which the same tone increases in power while being prolonged; (2) that in which succeeding tones are each sounded more strongly than the preceding one. The first variety is possible only on instruments giving forth a tone which can be varied *after it begins.* Thus *e.g.,* the human voice, the violin, the organ enclosed in a swell box, and certain wind instruments, are all capable of sounding a tone softly at first and gradually increasing the volume until the maximal point of power has been reached. But on the piano, organ not enclosed in a swell-box, kettle drum, etc., the power of the tone cannot be varied after the tone has once been sounded, and a *crescendo* effect is therefore possible only in a *passage*, in rendering which each succeeding tone is struck more forcibly than its immediate predecessor. This second variety of *crescendo* offers a means of dramatic effect which may be employed most strikingly, as *e.g.*, when a long passage begins very softly and increases in power little by little until the utmost resources of the instrument or orchestra have been reached. A notable example of such an effect is found in the transition from the third to the fourth movements of the Beethoven Fifth Symphony.

The difference between *sforzando, rinforzando,* and *crescendo* should now be noted: *sforzando* indicates that a single tone or chord is to be louder; *rinforzando,* that an entire passage is to be louder, beginning with its first tone; but *crescendo* indicates that there is to be a gradual increase in power, this increase sometimes occurring during the sounding of a single tone, but more often in a passage.

125. Certain *combinations of the word crescendo* with other words are so common that they should be especially noted. Among these are:

Crescendo al fortissimo — keep on gradually increasing in power until the fortissimo (or very loud) point has been reached.
Crescendo subito — increase in power suddenly (or rapidly).
Crescendo poco a poco — increase in power very, very gradually.
Crescendo poi diminuendo — first increase, then diminish the tone.
Crescendo e diminuendo — same as *cresc. poi dim.*
Crescendo molto — increase in power very greatly.
Crescendo ed animando poco a poco — growing gradually louder in tone and quicker in *tempo*.
Crescendo ed affrettando — gradually louder and faster.
Crescendo poco a poco sin al fine — crescendo gradually even up to the very end.

126. *Decrescendo* (*decresc.* or ══▶) means a gradual diminishing of the tone. It is the opposite of *crescendo*. The word *diminuendo* is synonymous with *decrescendo*.

Decrescendo (or *diminuendo*) *al pianissimo* means — decrease gradually in power until the *pianissimo* (or very soft) point is reached.

127. A number of *terms referring to both softer tone and slower tempo* are in use. The most common of these are: — mancando, moriente,[1] morendo, perdendo (from *perdere* — to lose), *perdendosi, calando*, and *smorzando*.[2] Such expressions are usually translated — "gradually dying away."

128. In piano music the abbreviation *Ped.* indicates that the damper pedal (the one at the right) is to be depressed, while the sign ✳ shows that it is to be released. In many modern editions this depression and release of the damper pedal are more accurately indicated by the sign └──┐.

The term *senza sordini* is also occasionally found in old editions, indicating that the damper pedal is to be depressed, while *con sordini* shows that it is to be released. These expressions are taken from a usage in music for stringed instruments, in which the term *con sordini* means that the mute (a small clamp of metal, ivory or hardwood) is to be affixed to the bridge, this causing a modification in both power and quality of the tone. The damper on the piano does not in any way correspond to the mute thus used on stringed instruments, and the terms above explained as sometimes occurring in piano music are not to be recommended, even though Beethoven used them in this sense in all his earlier sonatas.

129. The words *una corda* (lit. — one string) indicate that the "soft pedal" (the one at the left) is to be depressed, while the words *tre corde* (lit. three strings) or *tutte le corde* (all the strings) show that the same pedal is to be released. These expressions refer to the fact that on grand pianos the "soft pedal" when depressed moves the hammers to one side so that instead of striking three strings they strike only two (in the older pianos only one, hence *una corda*), all three strings (*tre corde*) being struck again after the release of the pedal.

130. Other terms relating either directly or indirectly to the subject of dynamics are:

Con amore — with tenderness.
Con bravura — with boldness.
Con celerita — with rapidity.
Con delicatezza — with delicacy.
Con energia — with energy.
Con espressione — with expression.

---

[1] Both *moriente* and *morendo* mean literally — *dying*.
[2] From *smorzare* (It.) — to extinguish.

Con forza — with force.

Con fuoco — with fire and passion.

Con grand' espressione — with great expression.

Con grazia — with grace.

Con malinconia — with melancholy.

Con passione — with passion.

Con spirito — with spirit.

Con tenerezza — with tenderness.

Delicato — delicately.

Dolce — sweetly, gently.

Dolcissimo — most sweetly.

Dolce e cantabile — gently and with singing tone.

Dolente ⎫
Doloroso ⎬ plaintively or sorrowfully.

Espressivo — expressively.

Grandioso — grandly, pompously.

Grazioso — gracefully.

Giocoso — humorously, (cf. jocose).

Giojoso — joyfully, (cf. joyous).

Lacrimando, lacrimoso — sorrowfully.

Legato — smoothly.

Leggiero — lightly.

Leggierissimo — most lightly; almost a staccato.

Lusingando — caressingly, coaxingly, tenderly.

Maesta, maestoso — majestically.

Martellando, martellato — strongly accented, (*lit.* — hammered).

Marziale — martial — war-like.

Mesto — pensively.

Mezzo voce — with half voice.

Misterioso — mysteriously.

Parlando — well accented or enunciated; applied to melody playing. (The word parlando means literally — speaking.)

Pastorale — in simple and unaffected style, (lit. — pastoral, rural).

Pomposo — pompously.

Precipitoso — precipitously.

Recitativo — well enunciated. (This meaning applies only in instrumental music in which a melody is to stand out above the accompaniment. For def. of recitative in vocal music, see p. 78.)

Risoluto — firmly, resolutely.

Scherzando, scherzoso, etc. — jokingly. These terms are derived from the word *scherzo* meaning *a musical joke.*

Semplice — simply.

Sempre marcatissimo — always well marked, *i.e.*, strongly accented.

Sentimento — with sentiment.

Solenne — solemn.

Sotto voce — in subdued voice.

Spiritoso — with spirit.

Strepitoso — precipitously.
Tranquillo — tranquilly.
Tristamente — sadly.

131. Many other terms are encountered which on their face sometimes seem to be quite formidable, but which yield readily to analysis. Thus *e.g., crescendo poco a poco al forte ed un pochettino accelerando,* is seen to mean merely — "increase gradually to *forte* and accelerate a very little bit." A liberal application of common sense will aid greatly in the interpretation of such expressions.

CHAPTER XIV

TERMS RELATING TO FORMS AND STYLES

132. A *form* in music is a specific arrangement of the various parts of a composition resulting in a structure so characteristic that it is easily recognized by the ear. Thus *e.g.*, although every fugue is different from all other fugues in actual material, yet the arrangement of the various parts is so characteristic that no one who knows the *fugue form* has any doubt as to what kind of a composition he is hearing whenever a fugue is played. The word *form* is therefore seen to be somewhat synonymous with the word *plan* as used in architecture; it is the structure or design underlying music. Examples of form are the canon, the fugue, the sonata, etc.

Speaking broadly we may say that *form* in any art consists in the placing together of certain parts in such relations of proportion and symmetry as to make a unified whole. In music this implies unity of tonality and of general rhythmic effect, as well as unity in the grouping of the various parts of the work (phrases, periods, movements) so as to weld them into one whole, giving the impression of completeness to the hearer.

133. The primal *basis of form* is the repetition of some characteristic effect, and the problem of the composer is to bring about these repetitions in such a way that the ear will recognize them as being the same material and will nevertheless not grow weary of them. This is accomplished by varying the material (cf. thematic development), by introducing contrasting material, and by choice of key.

134. The student should note at the outset of this topic the *difference in meaning between* the terms *form* and *style:*

A *form* is a plan for building a certain definite kind of composition, but a *style* is merely a manner of writing.   Thus *e.g.*, the *fugue* is a *form* — *i.e.*, it is a plan, which although capable of variation in details, is yet carried out fairly definitely in every case; but *counterpoint* is merely a *style* or manner of writing (just as Gothic architecture is a style of building), which may be cast into any one of several *forms*.

135. The material found in the following sections is an attempt to explain in simple language certain terms relating to *forms* and *styles* which are in common use; in many cases the definition is too meagre to give anything but a very general idea, but it is hoped that the student will at least be set to thinking and that he will eventually be led to a more detailed and scholarly study of the subject. (The article "Form" and the separate articles under each term here defined, as found in Grove's Dictionary, are especially recommended. For examples of the various forms described, see also Mason and Surette — "The Appreciation of Music," Supplementary Volume.)

136. In a very general way there may be said to be *two styles of musical composition*, the monophonic (or homophonic) — the one-voiced — and the polyphonic — the many voiced. The polyphonic[1] style antedates the monophonic historically.

137. In *monophonic music* there is one voice which has a pronounced melody, the other voices (if present) supporting this melody as a harmonic (and often rhythmic) background. An example of this is the ordinary hymn-tune with its melody in the highest part, and with three other voices forming a "four-part harmony."   The sonata, symphony, opera, modern piano piece, etc., are also largely *monophonic*, though polyphonic passages by way of contrast are often to be found.

---

[1] Polyphonic music flourished from 1000 A.D. to about 1750 A.D., the culmination of the polyphonic period being reached in the music of Johann Sebastian Bach (1685–1750). Haydn, Mozart, Beethoven, and the later writers have used the monophonic style more than the polyphonic, although a combination of the two is often found, as *e.g.*, in the later works of Beethoven.

138. In *polyphonic music* each voice is to a certain extent melodically interesting, and the "harmony" is the result of combining several melodies in such a way as to give a pleasing effect, instead of treating a melody by adding chords as an accompaniment or support. Counterpoint, canon, round, fugue, etc., are all *polyphonic* in style. The word *contrapuntal* is often used synonymously with *polyphonic*.

(Sections 139 to 143 relate especially to terms describing polyphonic music.)

139. *Counterpoint* is the art of adding one or more parts or melodies to a given melody, the latter being known as the "cantus firmus," or subject. It may therefore be broadly defined as "the art of combining melodies."

The word *counterpoint* comes from the three words "*punctus contra punctum,*" meaning "point against point." The word point as here used refers to the *punctus* — one of the neumae of the mediaeval system, these neumae being the immediate predecessors of modern notes.

Both vocal and instrumental music have been written in contrapuntal style. The familiar two- and three-part "inventions" by Bach are excellent examples of instrumental counterpoint, while such choruses as those in "The Messiah" by Handel illustrate the highest type of vocal counterpoint.

140. *Imitation* is the repetition by one part, of a subject or theme previously introduced by another part. If the imitation is exact, the term *strict imitation* is applied, but if only approximate, then the term *free imitation* is used in referring to it. The repetition need not have the exact pitches of the subject in order to be *strict;* on the contrary the imitation is usually at the interval of an octave, or a fifth, or a second, etc. Fig. 57 shows an example of strict imitation in which the *third* part comes in an octave *lower* than the first part.

141. A *canon* is a contrapuntal composition in the style of strict imitation, one part repeating exactly (but at any interval) what another part has played or sung. The term "canonic style" is sometimes applied to music in which the imitation is not exact. An example of three-part canon is given in Fig. 57.

CANON IN THREE VOICES, IN THE UNISON AND OCTAVE

Fig. 57. MOZART

The word *canon* means *law*, and was applied to this particular form of composition because the rules relating to its composition were invariable. It is because of this non-flexibility that the *canon* is so little used as a form at the present time: the modern composer demands a plan of writing that is capable of being varied to such an extent as to give him room for the exercise of his own particular individuality of conception, and this the *canon* does not do. For this same reason too the fugue and the sonata have successively gone out of fashion and from Schumann down to the present time composers have as it were created their own forms, the difficulty in listening arising from the fact that no one but the composer himself could recognize the form *as* a form because it had not been adopted to a great enough extent by other composers to make it in any sense universal. The result is that in much present-day music it is very difficult for the hearer to discover any trace of familiar design, and the impression made by such music is in consequence much less definite than that made by music of the classic school. It is probable that a reaction from this state of affairs will come in the near future, for in any art it is necessary that there should be at least enough semblance of structure to make the art work capable of standing as a universal thing rather than as the mere temporary expression of some particular composer or of some period of composition.

142. The common *school round* is an example of canon, each voice repeating exactly what the first voice has sung, while this first voice is going on with its melody. The *round* is therefore defined as a variety of canon in which the imitation is always in unison with the subject.

143. The *fugue* (Latin, *fuga* = flight) is a form of contrapuntal composition in which the imitation is always in the dominant key, *i.e.*, a fifth above or a fourth below. The imitation (called "the answer") may be an exact repetition of the subject (sometimes called "the question"), but is usually not so.

The *fugue* differs from the canon also in that the subject is given in complete form before the answer begins, while in the canon the imitation begins while the subject is still going on. The *fugue* is not nearly so strict in form as the canon and gives the composer much greater opportunity for expressing musical ideas. A canon may be perfect in *form* and yet be very poor music; this same statement might of course be made about any form, but is especially true in the stricter ones.

CHAPTER XV

TERMS RELATING TO FORMS AND STYLES (*Continued*)

(Sections 144 to 160 relate particularly to terms used in descriptions of *monophonic* music[1].)

144. A *phrase* is a short musical thought (at least two measures in length) closing with either a complete or an incomplete cadence. The typical *phrase* is four measures long. The two-measure *phrase* is often called *section*. The word *phrase* as used in music terminology corresponds with the same word as used in language study.

145. A *period* is a little piece of music typically eight measures long, either complete in itself or forming one of the clearly defined divisions of a larger form. The *period* (when complete in itself) is the smallest monophonic form.

The essential characteristic of the *regular period* is the fact that it usually consists of two balanced phrases (often called *antecedent* and *consequent* or *thesis* and *antithesis*), the first phrase giving rise to the feeling of incompleteness (by means of a cadence in another key, deceptive cadence, etc.,) the second phrase giving the effect of completeness by means of a definite cadence at the close.

The second half of the period is sometimes a literal repetition of the first half, in all respects except the cadence, but in many cases too it is a repetition of only one of the elements — rhythm, intervals, or general outline. Figs. 58 and 59 show examples of both types. The principle almost invariably holds that the simpler the music (cf. folk-tunes) the more obvious the form of the period, while the more complex the music, the less regular the period.

---

[1] There is a very pronounced disagreement among theorists as to what terms are to be used in referring to certain forms and parts of forms and it seems impossible to make a compromise that will satisfy even a reasonable number. In order to make the material in this chapter consistent with itself therefore it has been thought best by the author to follow the terminology of some single recognized work on form, and the general plan of monophonic form here given is therefore that of the volume called *Musical Form*, by Bussler-Cornell.

Fig. 58.   MOZART

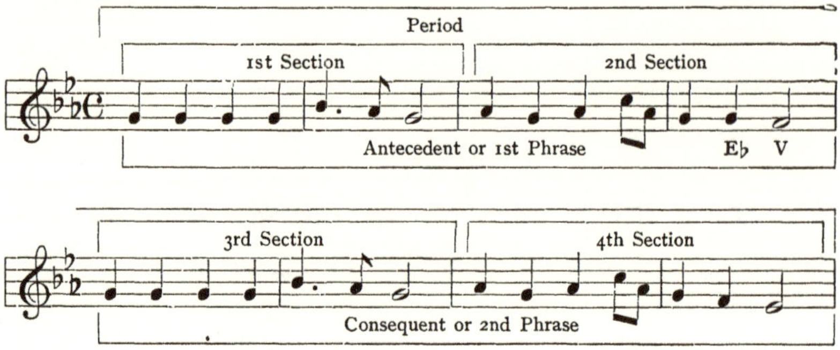

Fig. 59.   SCHUBERT

146. The *primary forms* are built up by combining two or more periods.

The *small two-part primary form* (often called *song-form* or *Lied-form*) consists of two periods so placed that the second constitutes a consequent or antithesis to the first. The second half of this second period is often exactly the same as the second half of the first period, thus binding the two periods together into absolute unity. The theme of the choral movement of the Ninth Symphony (Beethoven) quoted below is a perfect example of this form. Other examples are "Drink to Me Only With Thine Eyes," and "The Last Rose of Summer."

                                                                         BEETHOVEN

The *small three-part primary form* is like the two-part primary form except that it has a section of contrasting material interpolated between the two periods.   This middle part is usually an eight-measure phrase.

The *large two- and three-part primary forms* usually have sixteen-measure periods instead of eight-measure ones, but are otherwise similar in construction.

These various *primary forms* are used in constructing many varieties of compositions, among them the *theme and variations*, the *polka*, the *waltz*, the *march*, etc., as well as most of the shorter movements in sonatas, quartets, etc.   They are used in vocal music also, but are less apt to be regular here because the form of vocal music is largely dependent upon the structure of the text.

147. A *theme* is a fragment of melody used as the subject of a fugue, as the basis of the development section in "sonata form," etc.   Sometimes it is a complete tune (often in period form), on which variations are made, as *e.g.*, in the familiar *theme and variations*.

148. *Thematic development* consists in taking a short theme (or several short themes) and by means of transposition, interval expansion and contraction, rhythmic augmentation and diminution, inversion, tonality changes, etc., building out of it a lengthy composition or section of a composition.   Fig. 60 *b, c, d, e,* and *f* show how the theme given in Fig. 60 (*a*) may be varied in a few of these ways.   There are hundreds of other fashions in which this same theme might be varied without destroying its identity.   For other examples of thematic development see the development section of Sonata Op. 31, Sec. 3, as analyzed in Appendix E.

Fig. 60.

Original theme   Transposition

(c)
Interval expansion

(d)
Rhythmic augmentation

(e)
Rhythmic diminution

(f)
Inversion

For further illustrations of development in the case of this same theme, see — Christiani — The Principles of Expression in Pianoforte playing, p. 144, ff. from which the foregoing themes have been adapted.

149. A *rondo* is an instrumental composition (in homophonic style) in which a certain theme appears several times almost always in the same form (*i.e.*, not thematically varied), the repetitions of this theme being separated by contrasting material.

The *rondo* is the oldest of the larger monophonic forms and has been used in many different ways, but perhaps its most characteristic construction is as follows: (1) Principal subject; (2) second subject in dominant key; (3) principal subject; (4) third subject; (5) first subject again; (6 second subject, in *tonic key;* (7) coda (or ending).

The student should note particularly the problem of repetition and contrast (mentioned in Sec. 134) as here worked out, as the rondo was the first monophonic form in which this matter was at all satisfactorily solved, and its construction is especially interesting because it is readily seen to be one of the direct predecessors of the highest form of all — the sonata. Examples of rondos may be found in any volume of sonatas or sonatinas.

150. A *suite* is a set of instrumental dances all in the same or in nearly related keys. The first dance is usually preceded by an introduction or prelude, and the various dances are so grouped as to secure contrast of movement — a quick dance being usually followed by a slower one.

The suite is interesting to students of the development of music as being the first form *in several movements* to be generally adopted by composers. It retained its popularity from the beginning of the seventeenth to the end of the eighteenth centuries, being finally displaced by the sonata, whose immediate predecessor it is thus seen to be.

The *suite* was formerly written for solo instrument only (harpsichord, clavichord, piano) but modern composers like Dvořák, Lachner, Moszkowski, and others have written suites for full orchestra also.

151. Among the dances commonly found in suites are the following:

Allemande — duple or quadruple measure.
Bolero — triple measure.
Bourrée — duple or quadruple measure.
Chaconne — triple measure.
Courante — a very old dance in triple measure.
Csardas — Hungarian dance in duple or quadruple measure.
Gavotte — quadruple measure.
Gigue (or *jig*) — duple measure.
Habanera — Spanish dance in duple measure.
Minuet — slow dance in triple measure.
Mazurka — Polish dance in triple measure.
Polonaise — Polish dance in triple measure.
Rigaudon — lively dance in duple or triple measure.
Sarabande — triple measure.
Tarantella — swift Italian dance in sextuple measure.

The *allemande* is especially interesting to students of music form because of its relation to the sonata, it being the prototype of the sonata-allegro (*i.e.*, the first movement of the sonata). The *sarabande* and *courante* are likewise interesting as the prototypes of the second movement, and the *bouree*, *minuet*, etc., for their connection with the third movement.

152. The *scherzo* (lit. musical joke) is a fanciful instrumental composition. It was used by Beethoven as the third movement of the sonata instead of the more limited minuet, but is also often found as an independent piece.

153. A *sonata* is an instrumental composition of three or more movements (usually four), the first and last of which are

almost always in rapid tempo.   Each of these movements is a
piece of music with a unity of its own, but they are all merged
together in a larger whole with a broad underlying unity of
larger scope.   The composition receives its name from the
fact that its first movement is cast in *sonata-form.*   (See Sec.
157 for description of sonata-form.)

When the *sonata* has four movements, these are usually
arranged as follows:

1. A quick movement (*allegro, presto,* etc.), often preceded by a slower introduction.
2. A slow movement (*largo, andante, adagio,* etc.).
3. A minuet or scherzo, often with a trio added, in
   which case the part preceding the trio is repeated
   after the trio is played.
4. A quick movement — the finale, sometimes a rondo,
   sometimes another sonata-form, sometimes a theme
   with variations.

These movements are all in closely related keys, but in
a variety of contrasting rhythms.

154. A *trio* is a sonata for three instruments (such as
piano, violin, and cello), while a *quartet* is a sonata for four
instruments, the most common quartet combination being as
follows: First and second violins, viola, and violoncello.

The term *chamber music* is often applied to instrumental
music for trio, quartet, quintet, and other similar combinations
which are suitable for a small room rather than for a large
concert hall.

The words *trio* and *quartet* are also applied to vocal works for three and four
voices respectively, these having no relation whatsoever to the sonata as described
above.   The word *trio* is also applied to the middle section of minuets, scherzas,
marches, etc., the term originating in the old usage of writing this part for three instruments only.

155. A *concerto* is a sonata for a solo instrument with
orchestral accompaniment, the form being usually somewhat
modified so as to adapt it to a composition in which there must

necessarily be opportunity for a good deal of technical display. There are usually but three movements in the *concerto*.

The great majority of *concertos* are for piano and orchestra, but examples of concertos for violin, cello, flute, oboe, and other solo instruments (all with orchestral accompaniment) have also been written. A few modern composers have applied the term *concerto* to certain large organ works (with no orchestral accompaniment, the composition being written for just the one instrument), but this use of the word is so contrary to the accepted definition that it is hardly justifiable.

When a concerto is played on two pianos (without orchestra), this does not mean that there is no orchestral part, but that there is no orchestra to play it, and so the parts that should be played by the orchestral instruments have simply been arranged for a second piano (sometimes organ).

156. A *symphony* is a sonata for full orchestra. In general its construction is the same as that of the sonata, but it is usually of much larger proportions and has in it much greater variety of both tonal and rhythmic material. The symphony is generally conceded to be the highest type of instrumental music ever evolved.

The *symphony* was accepted as a standard form in the time of Haydn (1732–1809) and was developed enormously by Haydn himself, Mozart (1756–1791), and Beethoven (1770–1827), reaching perhaps its highest point in the famous "Nine Symphonies" of the last-named composer. Later symphony writers whose works are at present being performed include Schumann, Tschaikowsky, and Dvořák.

The word *symphony* was formerly used synonymously with *ritornelle*, both words being applied to instrumental interludes between parts of vocal works, but this usage has now entirely disappeared.

157. *Sonata-form* (sometimes called *sonata-allegro*) is a plan for the construction of instrumental music (sonatas, quartets, symphonies, etc.), in which three rather definite divisions always occur, the third division being a more or less literal repetition of the first.

These *three parts of sonata-form* with their usual subdivisions are:

I Exposition
    (1) Principal theme (or first subject).
    (2) Link-episode (or modulation group).
    (3) Secondary theme (or song group), always in a nearly related key.
    (4) Closing group.
    (5) Coda.

II DEVELOPMENT SECTION

Treating the themes introduced in the exposition in an almost infinite variety of fashions, according to the principles of thematic development. (See Sec. 148).

III. RECAPITULATION (OR REPRISE)

Consisting essentially of the same subdivisions found in the *exposition*, but differing from this first section in one essential point, viz., that instead of stating the secondary theme in a *related* key, the entire recapitulation is in the *principal* key. This third section is always followed by a coda (which may either be very short or quite extended), bringing the whole movement to a more definite close.

The second part of *sonata-form* (the development section) is often the longest and most intricate of the three divisions, and it is at this point that the composer has an opportunity of displaying to the full his originality and inventive skill. It is principally because of this development section that the sonata is so far superior as a *form* to its predecessors. For an analyzed example of *sonata-form*, see Appendix E. The student is advised to take other sonatas and go through the first movements with a view to finding at least the three main divisions mentioned above. In some cases the form will of course be so irregular that all the parts indicated cannot be discovered, but the general outlines of the scheme will always be present.

158. A *sonatina*, as its name implies, is a little sonata. It differs from the sonata proper principally in having little or no development, the second section being of slight importance as compared with the corresponding section of a sonata.

A *grand sonata* is like an ordinary sonata in form, but is of unusually large dimensions.

159. *Program music* is instrumental music which is supposed to convey to the listener an image or a succession of images that will arouse in him certain emotions which have been previously aroused in the composer's mind by some scene, event, or idea. The clue to the general idea is often given at the beginning of the music in the form of a poem or a short description of the thing in the mind of the composer, but there are many examples in which there is no clue whatsoever except the title of the composition.

Program music represents a mean between *pure music* (cf. the piano sonata or the string quartet) on the one hand, and *descriptive music* (in which actual imitations of bird-calls, whistles, the blowing of the wind, the galloping of horses, the rolling of thunder, etc., occur), on the other. Most program music is written for the orchestra, examples being Liszt's "The Préludes," Strauss' "Till Eulenspiegel," etc.

160. A *symphonic poem* (or *tone poem*) is an orchestral composition of large dimensions (resembling the symphony in size), usually embodying the program idea. It has no prescribed form and seems indeed to be often characterized by an almost total lack of design, but there are also examples of symphonic poems in which the same theme runs throughout the entire composition, being adapted at the various points at which it occurs to the particular moods expressed by the *program* at those points.

The *symphonic poem* was invented by Liszt (1811–1886) and has since been used extensively by Strauss, Saint-Saëns and others. It came into existence as a part of the general movement which has caused the fugue and the sonata successively to go out of fashion, *viz.*, the tendency to invent forms which would not hamper the composer in any way, but would leave him absolutely free to express his ideas in his own individual way,

CHAPTER XVI

Terms Relating to Vocal Music

161. An *anthem* is a sacred choral composition, usually based on Biblical or liturgical[1] words. It may or may not have an instrumental accompaniment, and is usually written in four parts, but may have five, six, eight, or more.

The word *anthem* is derived from *antifona* (or *antiphona*), meaning a psalm or hymn sung responsively, *i.e.*, *antiphonally*, by two choirs, or by choir and congregation.

A *full anthem* is one containing no solo parts; a *solo anthem* is one in which the solo part is predominant over the chorus, while a *verse anthem* is one in which the chorus parts alternate with passages for concerted solo voices (*i.e.*, trios, quartets, etc.).

162. A *capella* (sometimes spelled *cappella*) or *alla capella music* is part-singing (either sacred or secular) without accompaniment.

This term means literally " in chapel style," and refers to the fact that in the early days of the church all singing was unaccompanied.

163. A *motet* is a sacred choral composition in contrapuntal style. It has no solo parts, thus corresponding to the madrigal (q.v.) in secular music. The motet is intended for *a capella* performance, but is often given with organ accompaniment.

164. A *choral* is a hymn-tune of the German Protestant Church. It is usually harmonized in four voices. The *choral* (sometimes spelled *chorale*) is described as having "a plain melody, a strong harmony, and a stately rhythm." It differs from the ordinary English and American hymn-tune in being

---

[1] A *liturgy* is a prescribed form or method of conducting a religious service, and the parts sung in such a service (as *e.g.*, the holy communion, baptism, etc.), are referred to as the *musical* liturgy.

usually sung at a much slower tempo, and in having a pause at the end of each line of text.

165. The *mass* is the liturgy for the celebration of the Lord's Supper in the service of the Roman Catholic Church. As used in the terminology of music the word refers to the six hymns which are always included when a composer writes a musical *mass*, and which form the basis of the celebration of the Communion.[1] These six hymns are as follows:

> *Kyrie*
>
> *Gloria* (including the *Gratias agimus, Qui tollis, Quoniam, Cum Sancto Spirito*).
>
> *Credo* (including the *Et Incarnatus, Crucifixus,* and *Et Resurrexit*).
>
> *Sanctus* (including the *Hosanna*).
>
> *Benedictus.*
>
> *Agnus Dei* (including the *Dona nobis*).

The *requiem mass* is the "mass for the dead" and differs considerably from the ordinary mass. Both regular and requiem *masses* have been written by many of the great composers (Bach, Beethoven, Verdi, Gounod), and in many cases these *masses* are so complex that they are not practicable for the actual service of the Church, and are therefore performed only by large choral societies, as concert works.

166. A *cantata* is a vocal composition for chorus and soloists, the text being either sacred or secular. The accompaniment may be written for piano, organ, or orchestra.

When sacred in character the *cantata* differs from the oratorio in being shorter and less dramatic, in not usually having definite characters, and in being written for church use, while the oratorio is intended for concert performance.

When secular in subject the *cantata* differs from the opera in not usually having definite characters, and in being always rendered without scenery or action.

Examples of the *sacred cantata* are: Stainer's "The Crucifixion," Clough-Leighter's, "The Righteous Branch," and Gaul's "The Holy City." Examples of the *secular cantata* are: Bruch's "Armenius," Coleridge-Taylor's "Hiawatha."

167. An *oratorio* is a composition on a large scale for chorus, soloists, and orchestra, the text usually dealing with some religious subject. The *oratorio*, as noted above, is not

---

[1] It should be understood that this statement refers to the service called "the high mass" only, there being no music at all in connection with the so-called "low mass."

intended for the church service, but is written for concert performance.

168. An *opera* is a composition for vocal soloists, chorus, and orchestra, with characters, action, scenery, and dramatic movement. It is a drama set to music.

Grand opera is opera with a serious plot, in which everything is sung, there being no spoken dialog at all.

Opera comique is a species of opera in which part of the dialog is spoken and part sung. *Opera comique* is not synonymous with *comic opera*, for the plot of opera comique is as often serious as not. In fact the entire distinction between the terms *grand opera* and *opera comique* is being broken down, the latter term referring merely to operas first given at the Opera Comique in Paris, and the former term to those given at the Grand Opera House in the same city.

A *comic opera* is a humorous opera, the plot providing many amusing situations and the whole ending happily. It corresponds with the *comedy* in literature.

A *light opera* is one with an exceedingly trivial plot, in which songs, dances, and pretty scenery contribute to the amusement of the audience. The music is lively, but usually as trivial as the plot.

The term *music drama* was used by Wagner in referring to his own *operas*, and is also sometimes applied to other modern *operas* in which the dramatic element is supposed to predominate over the musical.

169. A *libretto* (lit. —little book) is the word-text of an opera, oratorio, cantata, or some other similar work.

170. *Recitative* is a style of vocal solo common to operas, oratorios, and cantatas, especially those written some time ago. Its main characteristic is that the word-text is of paramount importance, both rhythm and tone-progression being governed by rhetorical rather than by musical considerations.

Recitative undoubtedly originated in the intoning of the priest in the ritualistic service of the Church, but when applied to the opera it became an important means of securing dramatic effects, especially in situations in which the action of the play moved along rapidly. *Recitative* is thus seen to be a species of musical declamation.

In the early examples of *recitative* there was scarcely any accompaniment, often only one instrument (like the cello) being employed to play a sort of obbligato melody: when full chords were played they were not written out in the score, but were merely indicated in a more or less general way by certain signs and figures. (See "thorough-bass," p. 85, Sec. 200.)

But about the middle of the seventeenth century a slightly different style of *recitative* was invented, and in this type the orchestra was employed much more freely in the accompaniment, especially in the parts between the phrases of the text, but to some extent also to support the voice while singing. This new style was called *recitativo stromento* (*i.e.*, accompanied recitative), while the original type was called *recitativo secco* (*i.e.*, dry recitative).

During the last century the style of *recitative* has been still further developed by Gluck and Wagner, both of whom used the orchestra as an independent entity, with interesting melodies, harmonies and rhythms all its own, while the vocal part is a sort of obbligato to this accompaniment. But even in this latest phase of *recitative*, it is the word-text that decides the style of both melody and rhythm in the voice part. Fig. 61 shows an example of *dry recitative*, taken from "The Messiah."

171. *Aria* is likewise a style of vocal solo found in operas, etc., but its predominating characteristic is diametrically opposed to that of the recitative. In the *aria* the word-text is usually entirely subordinate to the melody, and the latter is often very ornate, containing trills, runs, etc.

The rendition of this ornate style of music is often referred to as "coloratura singing," but it should be noted that not all *arias* are coloratura in style.

The familiar solos from The Messiah — "Rejoice Greatly," and "The trumpet shall sound" are good examples of the aria style.

172. A *lied* or *art-song* is a vocal solo in which the text, the melody, and the accompaniment contribute more or less equally to the effect of the whole.

Strictly speaking the word *lied* means "a poem to be sung," and this meaning will explain at once the difference between the *lied* on the one hand, and the Italian recitative and aria on the other, for in the *lied* the text is of great importance, but the music is also interesting, while in the recitative the text was important but the music very slight, and in the aria the text was usually inconsequential while the music held the center of interest.

The most pronounced characteristic of the *lied* is the fact that it usually portrays a single mood, sentiment, or picture, thus differing from the ballad, which is narrative in style. It will be noted that this "single mood, or sentiment, or picture" was originally conceived by the poet who wrote the word-text, and that the composer in writing music to this text has first tried to get at the thought of the poet, and has then attempted to compose music which would intensify and make more vivid that thought. This intensification of the poet's thought comes as often through the rhythm, harmony, and dynamics of the accompaniment as through the expressiveness of the voice part.

The style of song-writing in which each verse is sung to the same tune is called the "strophe form," while that in which each verse has a different melody is often referred to as the "continuous" or "through-composed" form (Ger. durch-componiert).

173. A *ballad* was originally a short, simple song, the words being in narrative style, *i.e.*, the word-text telling a story. In the earlier *ballads* each verse of the poem was usually sung to the same tune (strophe form), but in the *art-ballad* as developed by Loewe and others the continuous style of composition is employed, this giving the composer greater opportunities of making vivid through his music the events described by the poem. These later *ballads* are in consequence neither "short" nor "simple" but compare in structure with the lied itself.

174. A *folk-song* is a short song sung by and usually originating among the common people. Its dominant characteristic is usually *simplicity*, this applying to word-text, melody, and accompaniment (if there is one). The text of the *folk-song* is usually based on some event connected with ordinary life, but there are also many examples in which historical and legendary happenings are dealt with. Auld Lang Syne, and Comin' thru the Rye, are examples of *folk-songs*.

There has been some difference of opinion as to whether a song, the composer of which is known, can ever constitute a real *folk-song:* recent writers seem to be taking the sensible view of the matter, viz.: that if a song has the characteristics of a folk- rather than an art-song, and if it remains popular for some time among the common people, then it is just as much a *folk-song* whether the composer happens to be known or not.

175. A *madrigal* is a secular vocal composition having from three to eight parts. It is in contrapuntal style, like the motet, and is usually sung a capella.

176. A *glee* is a vocal composition in three or more parts, being usually more simple in style than the madrigal, and sometimes having more than one movement. The *glee* may be either gay or sad in mood, and seems to be a composition peculiar to the English people.

177. A *part-song* is a composition for two or more voices, (usually four) to be sung a capella. It is written in monophonic rather than in polyphonic style, thus differing from the madrigal and glee. Morley's "Now is the Month of May- ing" is an example of the *part-song*, as is also Sullivan's "O Hush Thee, My Baby." The term *part-song* is often loosely applied to glees, madrigals, etc.

CHAPTER XVII

RHYTHM, MELODY, HARMONY AND INTERVALS

178. The *four elements* commonly attributed to music (in the order of their development) are: Rhythm, Melody, Harmony, and Timbre (or tone-color).

179. *Rhythm* is the regular recurrence of accent. In music it is more specifically the regular recurrence of groups of accented and non-accented beats (or pulses)— according to some specified measure-system. Since rhythm implies continuity, there must usually be at least two such measure groups in order to make musical rhythm possible. (See p. 44, Sec. 97.)

180. A *melody* is a succession of single tones of various pitches so arranged that the effect of the whole will be unified, coherent, and pleasing to the ear.

The soprano part of hymn-tunes and other simple harmonized compositions is often referred to as "the melody."

181. *Harmony* is the science of chord construction and combination.

The term *harmony* refers to tones sounding simultaneously, *i.e.*, to *chords*, as differentiated from tones sounding consecutively, as in melody. The word *harmony* may therefore be applied to any group of tones of different pitches sounded as a chord, although specifically we usually refer to a *succession* of such chords when we speak of "harmony." It is possible to use the same combination of tones in either melody or harmony; in fact these two elements as applied to modern music have developed together and the style of present-day melody is directly based upon the development that has recently taken place in harmonic construction.

Harmony (as contrasted with *counterpoint*) first began to be an important factor in music about 1600 A. D., *i.e.*, at the time when opera and oratorio came into existence, when form was established, and when our modern major and minor scales were adopted. Before this practically all music was composed on a contrapuntal basis.

182. *Timbre* is that peculiar quality of sound which enables one to distinguish a tone produced by one instrument (or

voice) from a tone produced by an equal number of vibrations on another instrument.

The word *timbre* is synonymous with the terms *quality of tone,* and *tone quality* (Ger. — Klang-farbe), the excuse for using it being that it expresses adequately in one word an idea that in our language takes at least two: this excuse would disappear (and incidentally a much-mispronounced word would be eliminated) if the single word *quality* were to be adopted as the equivalent of *timbre.* Thus, *e.g.,* the soprano voice singing c′ has a *quality* different from the contralto voice singing the same tone.

(The remainder of this chapter and all of Chapter XVIII deal with terms commonly encountered in the study of *harmony.* Courses in this subject usually begin with a study of scales, but since this subject has already been somewhat extensively treated, this chapter will omit it, and will begin with the next topic in harmony study, viz. — the interval.)

183. An *interval* is the relation of two tones with regard to pitch. If the two tones are sounded simultaneously the result is an *harmonic interval,* but if sounded consecutively the result is a *melodic interval.* Fig. 62 represents the pitches f′ and a′ as a harmonic interval, while Fig. 63 represents the same pitches arranged as a melodic interval.

Fig. 62.   Fig. 63.

184. In classifying intervals two facts should be constantly kept in mind:

(1) The *number name* of the interval (third, fifth, sixth, etc.), is derived from the order of letters as found in the diatonic scale. Thus the interval C—E is a *third* because E is the third tone from C (counting C as one) in the diatonic scale. C—G is a *fifth* because G is the fifth tone above C in the diatonic scale.

It should be noted however that the same *number-names* apply even though one or both letters of the interval are qualified by sharps, flats, etc. Thus *e.g.,* C—G♯ is still a *fifth,* as are also C♯—G♭ and C♭—G♯.

(2) In determining the *specific* name of any interval (*perfect* fifth, *major* third, etc.), the half-step and whole-step (often referred to respectively as *minor*

second, and *major second)* are used as units of measurement.

The *half-step* is usually defined as "the smallest usable interval between two tones." Thus, C—C♯ is a *half-step,* as are also B—C, F—G♭, etc.

A *whole-step* consists of two half-steps. C—D is a *whole-step,* as are also B♭—C, E—F♯, F♯—G♯, G♭—A♭, etc.

The expressions *half-step* and *whole-step* are much to be preferred to *half-tone* and *whole-tone,* as being more clear and definite. Thus *e.g.,* the sentence "The two tones are a *half-step* apart" is much better than "The two tones are a *half-tone* apart."

185. A *prime* is the relation between two tones whose pitches are properly represented by the same degree of the staff.

A *perfect prime* is one whose tones have the same pitch. Middle C sounded by piano and violin at the same time would offer an example.

An *augmented prime* is one whose second tone is one half-step higher than the first. Ex. C—C♯.

186. A *second* is the relation between two tones whose pitches are properly represented by adjacent degrees of the staff. (The first line and first space are adjacent degrees, as are also the third line and fourth space.)

A *minor second* is one comprising one half-step. Ex. B—C.

A *major second* is one comprising two half-steps. Ex. B—C♯.

An *augmented second* is one comprising three half-steps. Ex. F—G♯.

187. A *third* is an interval comprising two seconds.

A *diminished third* has two minor seconds (*i.e.,* two half-steps). C—E♭♭.

A *minor third* has one minor and one major second (*i.e.,* three half-steps). C—E♭.

A *major third* has two major seconds (*i.e.,* four half-steps). C—E.

188. A *fourth* is an interval comprising three seconds.

A *diminished fourth* has two minor and one major
second. C♯—F.

A *perfect fourth* has one minor and two major seconds.
C—F.

An *augmented fourth* (tritone) has three major seconds.
C—F♯.

189. A *fifth* is an interval comprising four seconds.

A *diminished fifth* has two minor and two major seconds.
C—G♭.

A *perfect fifth* has one minor and three major seconds.
C—G.

An *augmented fifth* has four major seconds. C—G♯.

190. A *sixth* is an interval comprising five seconds.

A *minor sixth* has two minor and three major seconds.
C—A♭.

A *major sixth* has one minor and four major seconds.
C—A.

An *augmented sixth* has five major seconds. C—A♯.

191. A *seventh* is an interval comprising six seconds.

A *diminished seventh* has three minor and three major
seconds. C—B♭♭.

A *minor seventh* has two minor and four major seconds.
C—B♭.

A *major seventh* has one minor and five major seconds.
C—B.

192. An *octave* is an interval comprising seven seconds.

A *diminished octave* has three minor and four major
seconds. C—C♭.

A *perfect octave* has two minor and five major seconds.
C—C.

An *augmented octave* has one minor and six major seconds. C—C♯.

193. A *ninth* is usually treated as a second, a *tenth* as a
third, etc.   The interval of two octaves is often referred to as
a *fifteenth.*

194. If the major diatonic scale be written and the interval between each tone and the key-tone noted, it will be observed that the intervals are all either major or perfect.   See Fig. 64.

Fig. 64.

Perfect Prime   Major 2d   Major 3d   Perfect 4th   Perfect 5th   Major 6th   Major 7th   Perfect Octave

o step   1 step   2 steps   2½ steps   3½ steps   4½ steps   5½ steps   6 steps

In this connection also it will be noted that the interval next smaller than *major* is always *minor*, while that next smaller than *perfect* or *minor* is always *diminished:* but that the interval next larger than both *major* and *perfect* is *augmented*.

195. An interval is said to be *inverted* when the tone originally the upper becomes the lower.   Thus C—E, a major third, inverted becomes E—C, a minor sixth.

CHAPTER XVIII

Chords, Cadences, Etc.

196. A *chord* is a combination of several tones sounding together and bearing an harmonic relation to each other. The simplest chord is the *triad*, which consists of a fundamental tone called the *root*, with the third and fifth above it. C—E—G is a triad, as are also D—F—A, F—A—C, and G—B—D.

197. Triads are classified as *major, minor, diminished,* or *augmented.*

> A *major triad* has a major third and a perfect fifth, *i.e.*, it is a major third with a minor third on top of it. Ex. C—E—G.
>
> A *minor triad* has a minor third and a perfect fifth, *i.e.*, it is a minor third with a major third on top of it. Ex. C—E♭—G.
>
> A *diminished triad* has a minor third and a diminished fifth, *i.e.*, it is a minor third with another minor third on top of it. Ex. C—E♭—G♭.
>
> An *augmented triad* has a major third and an augmented fifth, *i.e.*, it is a major third with another major third on top of it. Ex. C—E—G♯.

198. A triad may be built on any scale-tone, but those on I, IV, and V, are used so much oftener than the others that they are often called the *common chords.* In referring to triads the Roman numerals are used to show on what scale-tone the triad is based, the size of the numeral (with other signs) indicating the kind of triad found on each tone of the scale. Thus *e.g.*, the large I shows that the triad on the first tone (in major) is a *major triad*, the small II shows that the

triad on the second tone is minor, etc.   The following figure
will make this clear.

Fig. 65.

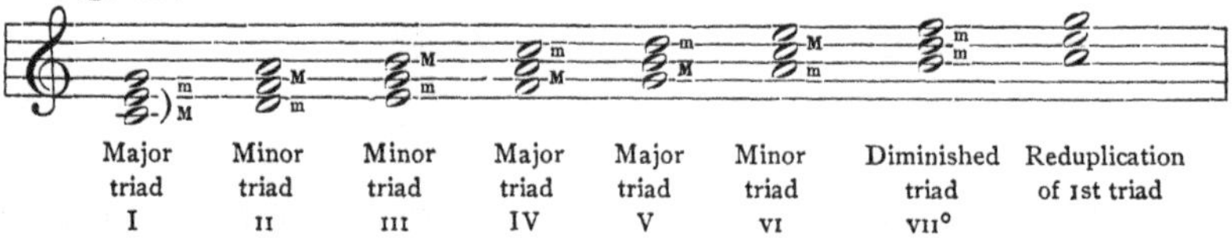

Major	Minor	Minor	Major	Major	Minor	Diminished	Reduplication
triad	triad	triad	triad	triad	triad	triad	of 1st triad
I	II	III	IV	V	VI	VII°	

The triads in the minor scale are as follows:

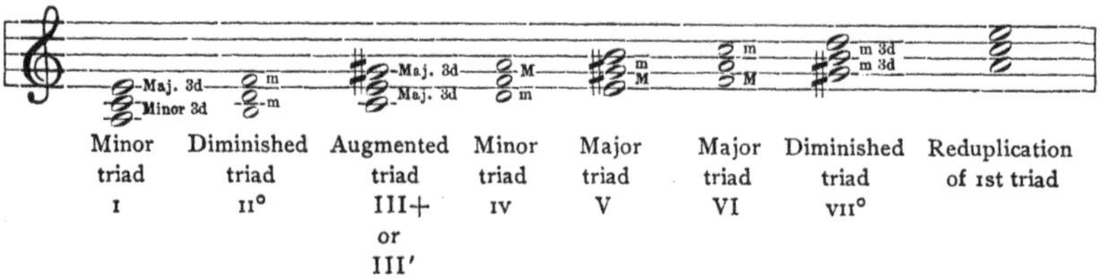

Minor	Diminished	Augmented	Minor	Major	Major	Diminished	Reduplication
triad	triad	triad	triad	triad	triad	triad	of 1st triad
I	II°	III+	IV	V	VI	VII°	
		or					
		III'					

199. A triad is said to be in *fundamental position* when its
root is the lowest tone. It is said to be in the *first inversion*
when the *third* is the lowest tone, and in the *second inversion*
when the fifth is the lowest tone. Thus *e.g.*, in Fig. 66 the
same chord (C—E—G) is arranged in three different positions,
at (*a*) in fundamental position, at (*b*) in the first inversion,
and at (*c*) in the second inversion.

Fig. 66.

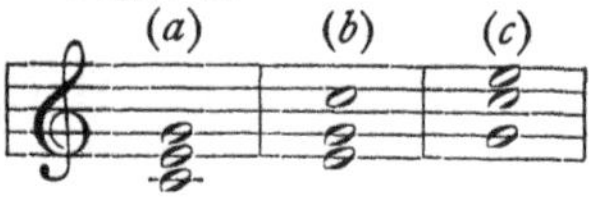

    (*a*)   (*b*)   (*c*)

200. When the root is not the bass note, figures are sometimes used to show what chord is to be played or written.
Thus, *e.g.*, the figure 6 over a bass note means that the note
given is the *third* of a chord, the root being found by going up
a sixth from the bass note: *i.e.*, the chord is to be sounded in
its first inversion. In the same way the figures ⁶₄ indicate
that the note given is the *fifth* of the chord, the root and fifth
being found by going up a sixth and a fourth from the note
given; *i.e.*, the chord is to be sounded in its second inversion.

The use of these and other similar figures and signs is called *figured bass* (or *thorough bass*) *notation*.   An example of a *figured bass* is given in Fig. 67.

Fig. 67.

Thorough bass notation was formerly used extensively in writing accompaniments to vocal works, the accompanist having to interpret the notes and signs given, and then to make up an interesting accompaniment as he went along.   Much of Handel's music was written in this way, but in modern editions of these works the chords have been printed in full and the signs omitted.

201. A *seventh chord* consists of a fundamental tone with its third, fifth, and seventh.   The fifth is sometimes omitted. A *ninth chord* consists of a fundamental with its third, fifth, seventh, and ninth.

202. A *cadence* is the close of a musical phrase: in melody it refers to the last two tones; in harmony to the last two chords.

The word *cadence* is derived from *cadere*, a Latin word meaning to *fall*, the reference being to the falling of the voice (*i.e.*, the dropping to the normal pitch) at the close of a sentence.

203. The most frequent cadence in harmony is that involving the chord on I preceded by the chord on V.   Because of its directness the cadence V—I is called the *authentic cadence*.

204. The most satisfactory form (to the ear) of the authentic cadence is that in which the highest voice (the soprano) of the final chord is the *root* of that chord.   When the final chord appears in this position the cadence is called *perfect*[1] *authentic*,

---

[1] Many theorists (including Durand in his monumental "Treatise on Harmony") consider the V—I cadence to be the only one which may legitimately be called *perfect*, but the majority of writers seem to take the view that either authentic or plagal cadence may be either perfect or imperfect, depending upon the soprano tone, as noted above.

and when the third or fifth of the chord appear in the soprano, the cadence is called *imperfect authentic*. Fig. 68 shows the chord G—B—D cadencing to C—E—G in three different ways. The first one (*a*) is called a *perfect authentic cadence*, but the last two (*c*) and (*d*) are *imperfect authentic*.

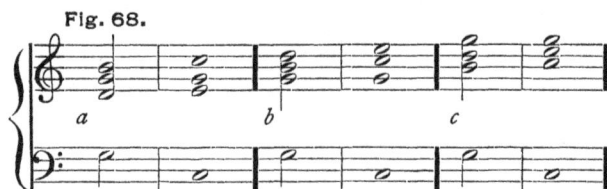

Fig. 68.

205. A *plagal cadence* is one in which the tonic chord is preceded by the sub-dominant chord (IV—I). The *plagal cadence* (sometimes called the *church cadence*, or *amen cadence*), like the authentic, is described as being *perfect* when the soprano of the tonic chord is the root of that chord, and *imperfect* when the soprano of the final chord is the third or fifth of that chord. Fig. 69 shows the chord F—A—C cadencing to C—E—G in three ways. The first one (*a*) is called a *perfect plagal cadence*, the last two are *imperfect plagal*.

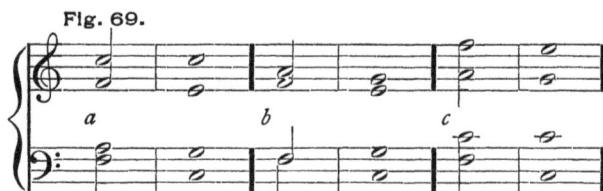

Fig. 69.

206. A *half-cadence* occurs when the dominant chord is used as the final chord of a phrase, and is immediately pre-. ceded by the tonic chord. This form is used to give variety in the course of a composition, but is not available at the end because it does not give a definite close in the tonic key. Fig. 70 shows the use of the *half-cadence* at the close of such a phrase.

Fig. 70.   BACH

Half Cadence

207. A *deceptive cadence* is the progression of the dominant chord to some other chord than the tonic, the word *deceptive* implying that the ear expects to hear V resolve to I and is deceived when it does not do so. The most common form of *deceptive cadence* is that in which V (or V⁷) resolves to VI. It is used to give variety, but as in the case of the half-cadence, is not available at the end of a composition. Fig. 71 gives an example.

Fig. 71.   WM. MATHER

Deceptive Cadence

208. A *sequence* is a succession of similar harmonic progressions, these resulting from a typical or symmetrical movement of the bass part. See Fig. 72.

Fig. 72.

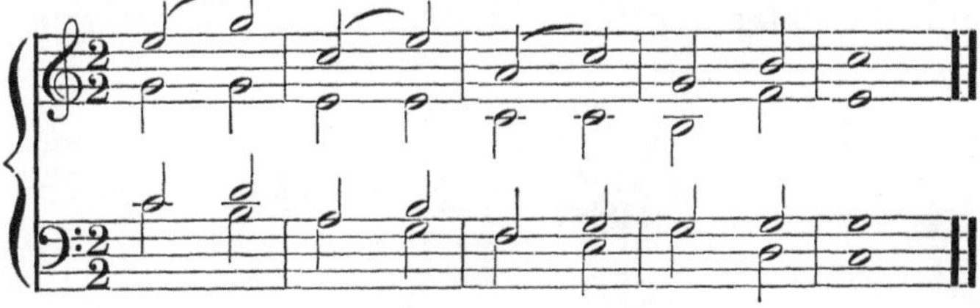

The word *sequence* is also applied to a succession of similar melodic progressions, as in Fig. 73.

Fig. 73.

209. *Modulation* is a change of key without any break in the continuity of chords or melody tones. *Harmonic modulations* are usually effected through the medium of a chord, some or all of whose tones are common to both keys. Examples of both *harmonic* and *melodic modulations* are shown in Figs. 74 and 75.

Fig. 74.

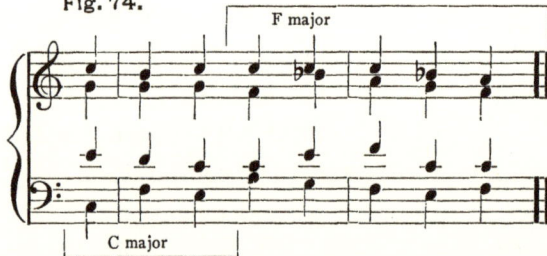

The chord most frequently used in modulating is the *dominant seventh*, *i.e.*, a seventh chord (see Sec. 201) on the dominant tone of the key. In the key of C this chord is G—B—D—F; in the key of D it is A—C♯—E—G; in the key of A♭ it is E♭—G—B♭—D♭, etc.

Fig. 75.

G . . . . to . . . . . . D

210. A *suspension* is the temporary substitution of a tone a degree higher than the regular chord-tone, this temporary tone being later replaced by the regular chord-tone. See Fig. 76 (*a*).

Fig. 76. (*a*)

211. A *retardation* is the temporary substitution of a tone a degree lower than the regular tone, this tone (as in the case of the suspension) being later replaced by the regular chord tone. See Fig. 77 (*a*).

Fig. 77. (*a*)

The "regular chord tone" to which both suspension and retardation resolve is called the *tone of resolution.*

212. The *anticipation* is a chord-tone introduced just before the rest of the chord to which it belongs is sounded. See Fig. 78 (*a*).

Fig. 78. (*a*)

213. A *pedal point* (or *organ point*) is a tone sustained through a succession of harmonic progressions, to the chords of some of which it usually belongs. The term *pedal point* originated in organ playing, (where the foot on a pedal can sustain a tone while the hands are playing a succession of harmonies), but as now used it may be applied to any kind of music. The dominant and tonic are the tones most often used in this way. See Fig. 79.

Fig. 79.   SCHUMANN

214. When the upper three voices of a four-voice composition are written close together (the soprano and tenor never appearing more than an octave apart), the term *close position* is applied.   But when the upper voices are not written close together, the term *open position* is applied.

215. By *transposition* is meant playing, singing, or writing a piece of music in some other key than the original.   Thus *e.g.*, if a song written in the key of G is too high in range for a soloist, the accompanist sometimes *transposes* it to a lower key (as F or E), thus causing all tones to sound a second or a third lower than they did when the same song was played in the original key.

CHAPTER XIX

Miscellaneous Terms

A battuta — with the beat; in strict rhythm.

A quatre mains — for four hands.

Accompagnamento — the accompaniment.

All unisono — in unison.

Alla breve — $\frac{2}{2}$ measure.

The term *alla breve* is also sometimes used as a tempo indication, to show a rate of speed so great that a half-note has a beat, *i.e.*, only two beats in a measure — hence twice as fast as before.

Alla capella — usually the same as a capella (see p. 76, Sec. 162) but sometimes *used* in the same sense as *alla breve*.

Alla marcia — in march style.

Alla zingara — in gypsy style.

Alt — see *in alt*.

Alto — the lowest female voice. Range approximately g—e."

The word *alto* is derived from the Latin word *altus*, meaning *high*, the term being formerly applied to the highest male voice, which originally sang (and still does so in many male choirs) the alto part.

Animato come sopra — in animated style as above.

Antiphony (*antiphonal*) — the responsive singing of two choirs, usually one at either end of the church, or at either side of the chancel.

Arabesque — an instrumental composition in light, somewhat fantastic style.

The term *arabesque* is derived from the word *Arabian*, and was originally applied to a style of decoration.

Arioso — in the style of an air or song, *i.e.*, a flowing, vocal style.

Attacca — attack the next division without any pause.

Attacca subito — same as *attacca*.

Attacca subito il seguente — attack at once that which follows.

Attack — the promptness or firmness with which a phrase is begun.

Bagpipe — A Scotch instrument on which the tone is produced by a combination of bellows and reeds. Its characteristic effect is the continuous sounding of a low tone (sometimes several tones) while the melody is being played on the higher reeds.

Barcarole (or *barcarolle*) — a boat song. Also applied to a vocal or instrumental composition in the style of the gondolier's boat song.

Baritone (or *barytone*) — the male voice having a range between that of the tenor and that of the bass. Approximate range G—g′.

Bass — the lowest male voice. Approximate range E—e′.

Basso — same as *bass*.

Berceuse — a cradle song.

Binary form — a form in two parts.

Binary measure — a measure having two beats.

Bis — twice. Used to indicate a repetition. (Rare.)

Brace — the sign used to join several staffs, showing that all tones represented on these staffs are to be performed together. The term is often used also in referring to the music written on staffs so joined; as — "Begin with the upper *brace*."

Broken chord — a chord whose tones are not all sounded simultaneously, as *e.g.*, in an accompaniment group.

Broken octave — an octave whose tones are sounded one at a time instead of simultaneously.

Cacophony — harsh, discordant, unpleasant, especially *incorrect* combinations of tones. The opposite of *euphony*.

Cadenza — A brilliant passage, usually in an instrumental composition, introduced just before the close of a movement. The *cadenza* was formerly improvised by the performer, (thus giving an opportunity of displaying his technical skill), but since Beethoven, composers have usually written their own *cadenzas*.

Cantabile — in a singing style.

Cantando — same as *cantabile*.

Canto — the highest voice part; *i.e.*, the soprano part.

Note the derivation of *canto*, *cantabile*, etc., from the Latin word *cantus*, meaning a *song*.

Carol — a hymn of joyful praise, usually sung in connection with Easter or Christmas festivities. The word *carol* meant originally *a dance*, hence the *happy* character of songs of this type.

Catch — a round set to humorous words.

Chromatic (noun) — a term somewhat loosely applied to any tone not belonging to the key as indicated by the signature. Many teachers are replacing the word *chromatic* in this sense with the term *intermediate tone*, this term being applicable whether the foreign tone is actually used for ornamental purposes as a *chromatic*, or to effect a modulation. Thus *e.g.*, "F♯ is the *intermediate tone* between F and G in the key of C."

Clavichord — an instrument with keys, resembling the square piano in appearance. The tone was produced by forcing wedge-shaped pieces of metal against the strings, thus setting them in vibration. The *clavichord* was one of the immediate predecessors of the piano, much of the music written by Bach being composed for it, although this music is now played on the modern piano.

Colla voce — with the voice: *i.e.*, play the accompaniment according to the soloist's performance rather than strictly according to the rhythm indicated in the score.

Colla parte — same as *colla voce*.

Coloratura — florid passages in singing. Also applied to the style of singing employed in rendering such passages. (See p. 79, Sec. 171.)

Consonance — A combination of tones agreeable to the ear and requiring no resolution to other tone-combinations in order to give the effect of finality. The major triad C—E—G is an example of a consonant chord.

Contralto — same as *alto*.

Con variazioni — with variations.

Direct — a sign (𝄈) placed at the end of the last staff on a page, to indicate what the first note on the next page is going to be. This sign is now practically obsolete.

Dirge — a funeral chant. The dirge is named from the first word of a chant used in the "office for the dead," which begins — *Dirige Domine, Deus meus, in conspectu tuo viam meam* (Direct, O Lord, My God, my way in Thy sight).

Discord — an ugly, unharmonious combination of tones.

Dissonance — a harmonic combination of tones giving rise to the feeling of incompleteness or unrest, and therefore requiring resolution to some other combination which has an agreeable or final feeling. (cf. consonance.) The diminished triad C–E♭–G♭ is an example of a dissonant chord.

Divisi — divided. An indication showing that the first violins, or the sopranos, or any other body of performers ordinarily sounding in unison are now to divide into two or more parts.

Duet — a composition for two performers. (From the It. word *due* — two.)

École — a school or style of composition or performance.

Etude — a study. Also an instrumental composition in the style of a study, but intended for artistic performance.

Euphony — agreeable tone combinations; the opposite of cacophony. (From the Greek word meaning *well-sounding*.)

Facile — easy.

Fanfare — a trumpet call.

Fantasia — An instrumental composition not based on any regular form.

Fiasco — a complete failure or breakdown.

This use of the word *fiasco* (which means in Italian a flask, or bottle) is said to have reference to the bursting of a bottle, the complete ruin of the bottle being compared with the complete failure of a performance.

Gamut — all the tones of a scale.

Glissando — playing a scale on the keyboard by drawing the finger along over the keys, thus depressing them in very rapid succession. The word is derived from the French word *glisser* — to glide.

Harpsichord — one of the immediate predecessors of the piano.

Humoresque — a capricious, fantastic composition. (Cf. *fantasia*.)

Idyl — a short, romantic piece of music in simple and unaffected style.

In alt — pitches in the first octave above the treble staff. Thus *e.g.*, "C in alt" is the C represented by the second added line above the treble staff.

In altissimo — pitches in the octave above the *alt* octave.

Instrumentation — see *orchestration*.

Interlude — a short movement between two larger movements.

Loco — place; *i.e.*, play as written. (See p. 15, Sec. 46.)

Lungo trillo — a long trill.

CHAPTER XX

MISCELLANEOUS TERMS (*Continued*)

Lyric — a short, song-like poem of simple character. Also applied to instrumental pieces of like character.

Maggiore — major.

Marcato il canto — the melody well marked; *i.e.*, subdue the accompaniment so that the melody may stand out strongly.

Melos — melody. This word *melos* is also applied to the peculiar style of vocal solo found in Wagner's music dramas. See *recitative* (p. 78, Sec. 170).

Mellifluous — pleasing; pleasant sounding.

Menuetto, menuet — same as *minuet*. (See p. 71, Sec. 151.)

Mezzo soprano — a woman's voice of soprano quality, but of somewhat lower compass than the soprano voice. Range approximately b to g."

Minore — minor.

Nocturne (sometimes spelled *nocturn, notturna, nokturne*, etc.) — a night piece; a quiet, melodious, somewhat sentimental composition, usually for piano solo.

Nuance — delicate shading; subtle variations in tempo and dynamics which make the rendition of music more expressive.

Obbligato (sometimes in_correctly spelled *obligato*) — an accessory melody accompanying harmonized music, (usually vocal music).

The word *obbligato* (It. *bound*, or *obliged*) refers to the fact that this is usually a melody of independent value, so important that it cannot be omitted in a complete performance.

Offertory (sometimes spelled *offertoire*, or *offertorium*) — a piece of music played or sung during the taking up of the offering in the church service. The word is often applied by composers to any short, simple piece of music (usually for organ) that is suitable for the above purpose.

Opus — work; used by composers to designate the order in which their compositions were written, as *e.g.*, Beethoven, Op. 2, No. 1.

Orchestration — the art of writing for the orchestra, this implying an intimate knowledge of the range, quality, and possibilities of all the orchestral instruments.

Ossia — or else; used most often to call the attention of the performer to a simpler passage that may be substituted for the original one by a player whose skill is not equal to the task he is attempting to perform.

Overture — (from *overt* — open) — an instrumental prelude to an opera or oratorio. The older *overtures* were independent compositions and bore no particular relation to the work which was to follow, but in modern music (cf. Wagner, Strauss, etc.), the *overture* introduces the principal themes that are to occur in the work itself, and the introduction thus becomes an integral part of the work as a whole. The word *overture* is sometimes applied to independent orchestral compositions that have no connection with vocal works, as the *Hebrides Overture* by Mendelssohn.

Pizzicato — plucked. A term found in music for stringed instruments, and indicating that for the moment the bow is not to be used, the tone being secured by *plucking* the string.

Polacca — a Polish dance in three-quarter measure.

Polonaise — same as *polacca*.

Postlude — (lit. after-play) — an organ composition to be played at the close of a church service.

Prelude — (lit. before-play) — an instrumental composition to be played at the beginning of a church service, or before some larger work (opera, etc.). The term is also applied to independent piano compositions of somewhat indefinite form. (Cf. *preludes* by Chopin, Rachmaninoff, etc.)

Prière — a prayer; a term often applied (especially by French composers) to a quiet, devotional composition for organ.

Quintole, quintuplet — a group of five notes to be performed in the time ordinarily given to four notes of the same value. There is only one accent in the group, this occurring of course on the first of the five tones.

Religioso, religiosamente — in a devotional style.

Requiem — the mass for the dead in the Roman Catholic service. It is so called from its first word *requiem* which means *rest*. (See p. 77, Sec. 165.)

Rhapsody — an irregular instrumental composition of the nature of an improvisation. A term first applied by Liszt to a series of piano pieces based on gypsy themes.

Ribattuta — a device in instrumental music whereby a two-note phrase is gradually accelerated, even to the extent of becoming a trill. (See Appendix E, p. 150, for an example.)

Ritornello, ritornelle — a short instrumental prelude, interlude, or postlude, in a vocal composition, as *e.g.*, in an operatic aria or chorus.

Schottische — a dance in two-quarter measure, something like the *polka*.

Sec, secco — dry, unornamented: applied to a style of opera recitative (see p. 78, Sec. 170), and also to some particular chord in an instrumental composition which is to be sounded and almost instantly dropped.

Score — a term used in two senses:

1. To designate some particular point to which teacher or conductor wishes to call attention; as *e.g.*, "Begin with the *lower score*, third measure." The word *brace* is also frequently used in this sense.

2. To refer to all the parts of a composition that are to be performed simultaneously, when they have been assembled on a single page for use by a chorus or orchestral conductor. The term *vocal score* usually means all chorus parts together with an accompaniment arranged for piano or organ, while the terms *full score* and *orchestral score* refer to a complete assemblage of *all parts*, each being printed on a separate staff, but all staffs being braced and barred together.

Senza replica, senza repetitione — without repetition; a term used in connection with such indications as *D.C., D.S.*, etc., which often call for the repetition of some large division of a composition, the term *senza replica* indicating that the smaller repeats included within the larger division are not to be observed the second time.

Serenade, serenata — an evening song.

Sextet — a composition for six voices or instruments.

Sextuplet — a group of six notes to be performed in the time ordinarily given to four of the same value. The sextuplet differs from a pair of *triplets* in having but one accent.

Simile, similiter — the same; indicating that the same general effect is to be continued.

Solfeggio, solfège — a vocal exercise sung either on simple vowels or on arbitrary syllables containing these simple vowel sounds. Its purpose is to develop tone quality and flexibility. These terms are also often applied to classes in sight-singing which use the sol-fa syllables.

Sopra — above.

Soprano — the highest female voice. Range approximately b—c.'''

Sostenuto — sustained or connected ; the opposite of *staccato*.

Sotto — under. *E.G.*, *sotto voce* — under the voice, *i.e.*, with subdued tone.

Solmization — sight-singing by syllable.

Stàccato — detached; the opposite of *legato*.

Subito — suddenly.

Tenor — the highest male voice. Range approximately d—c.''

Tenuto — (from *teneo*, to hold) — a direction signifying that the tones are to be prolonged to the full value indicated by the notes.

Toccata — a brilliant composition for piano or organ, usually characterized by much rapid staccato playing.

Triplet — a group of three tones, to be performed in the time ordinarily given to two of the same value. The first tone of the triplet is always slightly accented.

Tutti — (derived from *totus, toti*, Latin — all) — a direction signifying that all performers are to take part. Also used occasionally to refer to a passage where all performers do take part.

APPENDIX A

The History of Music Notation

Many conflicting statements have been made regarding the history and development of music writing, and the student who is seeking light on this subject is often at a loss to determine what actually did happen in the rise of our modern system of writing music. We have one writer for example asserting that staff notation was begun by drawing a single red line across the page, this line representing the pitch *f* (fourth line, bass staff), the *neumae* (the predecessors of our modern *notes*) standing either for this pitch *f*, or for a higher or lower pitch, according to their position *on* the line, or *above* or *below* it. "Another line," continues this writer, "this time of yellow color, was soon added above the red one, and this line was to represent c′ (middle C). Soon the colors of these lines were omitted and the *letters* F and C were placed at the beginning of each of them. From this arose our F and C clefs, which preceded the G clef by some centuries."[1]

Another writer[2] gives a somewhat different explanation, stating that the staff system with the use of clefs came about through writing a letter (C or F) in the margin of the manuscript and drawing a line from this letter to the neume which was to represent the tone for which this particular letter stood.

A third writer[3] asserts that because the alphabetical notation was not suitable for recording melodies because of its

---

[1] Elson — Music Dictionary, article, "Notation."
[2] Goddard — The Rise of Music, p. 177.
[3] Williams in Grove's Dictionary, article, "Notation."

inconvenience in sight-singing "points were placed at definite distances above the words and above and below one another." "In this system . . . . . everything depended on the accuracy with which the points were interspersed, and the scribes, as a guide to the eye, began to scratch a straight line across the page to indicate the position of one particular scale degree from which all the others could be shown by the relative distances of their points. But this was not found sufficiently definite and the scratched line was therefore colored red and a second line was added, colored yellow, indicating the interval of a fifth above the first."

It will be noted that all three writers agree that a certain thing happened, but as in the case of the four Gospels in the New Testament, not all the writers agree on details and it is difficult to determine which account is most nearly accurate in detail as well as in general statement. Communication was much slower a thousand years ago than now and ideas about new methods of doing things did not spread rapidly, consequently it is entirely possible that various men or groups of men in various places worked out a system of notation differing somewhat in details of origin and development but alike in final result. The point is that the development of musical knowledge (rise of part-writing, increased interest in instrumental music, etc.), demanded a more exact system of notation than had previously existed, just as the development of science in the nineteenth century necessitated a more accurate scientific nomenclature, and in both cases the need gave rise to the result as we have it to-day.

Out of the chaos of conflicting statements regarding the development of music notation, the student may glean an outline-knowledge of three fairly distinct periods or stages, each of these stages being intimately bound up with the development of *music* itself in that period. These three stages are:

(1) The Greek system, which used the letters of the alphabet for representing fixed pitches.

(2) The period of the neumae.

(3) The period of staff notation.

Of the Greek system little is known beyond the fact that the letters of the alphabet were used to represent pitches. This method was probably accurate enough, but it was cumbersome, and did not afford any means of writing "measured music" nor did it give the eye any opportunity of grasping the general outline of the melody in its progression upward and downward, as staff notation does. The Greek system seems to have been abandoned at some time preceding the fifth century. At any rate it was about this time that certain *accent marks* began to be written above the text of the Latin hymns of the church, these marks serving to indicate in a general way the progress of the melody. E.g., an upward stroke of the pen indicated a rise of the melody, a downward stroke a fall, etc. In the course of two or three centuries these marks were added to and modified quite considerably, and the system of notation which thus grew up was called "neume notation," the word *neume* (sometimes spelled *neuma*, or *pneuma*) being of Greek origin and meaning a *nod* or *sign*.

This system of neumes was in some ways a retrogression from the Greek letter system, for the neumes indicated neither definite pitches nor definite tone-lengths. But it had this advantage over the Greek system, that the position of the signs on the page indicated graphically to the eye the general direction of the melody, as well as giving at least a hint concerning the relative highness or lowness of each individual tone (the so-called *diastematic system*), and this was a great aid to the eye in singing, just as the relative highness and lowness of notes on the modern staff is of great value in reading music at the present time. Thus although the neumae did not enable one to sing a new melody at sight as our modern staff notation does, yet they served very well to recall to the eye the general outline of a melody previously learned by ear and therefore enabled the singer (the system was used for vocal music only) to differentiate between that particular melody and the dozens of others which he probably knew. Neume notation was used mostly in connection with the "plain-song melodies" of the Church, and since the words of these chants were sung as they would be pronounced in reading, the deficiency of the neume system in not expressing definite duration values was not felt. But later on with the rise of so-called "measured music" (cf. invention of opera, development of independent instrumental music, etc.), this lack was seen to be one of the chief disadvantages of the system.

The elements of neume-writing as given by Riemann in his Dictionary of Music are:

"(1) The signs for a single note: Virga (Virgula) and Punctus (Punctum). (2) The sign for a rising interval: Pes (Podatus). (3) The sign for a falling interval: Clinis (Flexa). (4) Some signs for special manners of performance: Tremula (Bebung), Quilisma (shake), Plica (turn), etc. The others were either synonyms of the above-named or combinations of them . . . ."

Since music in the middle ages was always copied by hand, it will readily be understood that these neumae were not uniform either in shape or size, and that each writer made use of certain peculiarities of writing, which, although perfectly intelligible to himself, could not readily be interpreted by others (cf. writing shorthand). Here then we observe the greatest weakness of the neume system — its lack of uniformity and its consequent inability accurately to express musical ideas for universal interpretation.

Examples of several neumes are given merely in order to give the beginner a general idea of their appearance.

Virga ♪ or ╱ . Punctus ✦ or ◗ . Pes ✓ or ∫ . Clinis ⌐ or ∧ .

As music grew more and more complex, and especially as writing in several parts came into use (cf. rise of organum, descant, and counterpoint), it became increasingly difficult to express musical ideas on the basis of the old notation, and numerous attempts were made to invent a more accurate and usable system. Among these one of the most interesting was that in which the words of the text were written in the spaces between long, parallel lines, placing the initial letters of the words *tone* and *semi-tone* at the beginning of the line to indicate the scale interval. An example will make this clear.

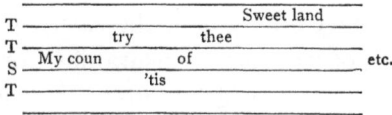

This indicated the precise melodic interval but did not give any idea of the rhythm, and the natural accents of the text were the only guide the singer had in this direction, as was the case in neume-notation and in early staff-notation also. Various other attempts to invent a more definite notation were made, but all were sporadic, and it was not until the idea of using the lines (later lines and spaces) to represent definite pitches, and writing notes of various shapes (derived from the neumae) to indicate relative duration-values — it was only when this combination of two elements was devised that any one system began to be universally used.

Just how the transition from *neume* to *staff* notation was made no one knows: it was not done in a day nor in a year but was the result of a gradual process of evolution and improvement. Nor is it probable that any one man deserves the entire credit for the invention of staff notation, although this feat is commonly attributed to an Italian monk named Guido d'Arezzo (approximate dates 995–1050). To this same monk we are indebted, however, for the invention of the syllables (UT, RE, MI, etc.) which (in a somewhat modified form) are so widely used for sight-singing purposes. (For a more detailed account of the transition to staff notation, see Grove, op. cit. article *notation*.) It will now be readily seen that our modern notation is the result of a combination of two preceding methods (the Greek letters, and the neumes) together with a new element — the staff, emphasizing the idea that *higher tones* are written *higher* on the staff then lower ones. The development of the neumes into notes of various shapes indicating relative time values and the division of the staff into measures with a definite measure signature at the beginning are natural developments of the earlier primitive idea.

In the system of "musica mensurabilis" or *measured music* which was inaugurated a little later, the *virga* (which had meanwhile developed into a square-headed neume) was adopted as the *longa* or long note, and the punctus in two of its forms as *breve* and *semibreve* (short and half-short). The longa is now extinct, but the modern form of the breve is still used as the double-whole-note, and the semibreve is our modern whole-note.

Red-colored notes were sometimes used to indicate changes in value and before long outline notes (called *empty notes*) came into use, these being easier to make than the solid ones. The transition from square- and diamond-shaped notes to round and oval ones also came about because of the greater facility with which the latter could be written, and for the same reason notes of small denomination were later "tied together" or *stroked*. This latter usage began about 1700 A.D.

It is interesting to find that when "measured music" was finally inaugurated there were at first but two measure-signatures, viz. — the circle, standing for three-beat measure (the so-called *perfect measure*) and the semi-circle (or broken circle) which indicated two-beat measure. Occasionally three-beat measure was indicated by three vertical strokes at the

beginning of the melody, while two-beat measure was shown
by two such strokes. Upon the basis of these two varieties
of measure, primitive in conception though they may have
been, has been built nevertheless the whole system now
employed, and in the last analysis all forms of measure now in
use will be found to be of either the two-beat or the three-beat
variety. The circle has disappeared entirely as a measure-
sign, but the broken circle still survives, and from it are derived the familiar signs 𝄴 and 𝄵, which are sometimes erroneously referred to as being the initial letter of our word *common*
(as used in the expression "common time"). The transition
from the older style of measure-signature to the present one
seems to have occurred during the century following the invention of opera, *i.e.*, from about 1600 to about 1700 A.D.

The rest came into use very soon after "measured music"
began to be composed and we soon find rests corresponding
with the various denominations of notes in use, viz.:

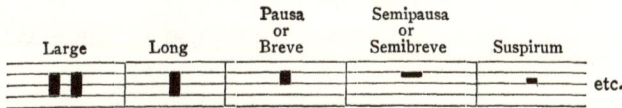

Large	Long	Pausa or Breve	Semipausa or Semibreve	Suspirum	
𝄰𝄰	𝄰	▪	▬	▪	etc.

The terms applied to these rests vary in different authori-
ties, but it will be noted that the *pausa, semi-pausa*, and *sus-
pirum* correspond respectively to the double-whole-rest, whole-
rest, and half-rest in use at present.

The bar and double bar may be developments of the
maxima rest (as some writers suggest) but are probably also
derived from the practice of drawing a line vertically through
the various parts of a score to show which notes belonged together, thus facilitating score reading. The bar may occasionally be found as early as 1500, but was not employed universally
until 1650 or later.

The number of lines used in the staff has varied greatly
since the time of Guido, there having been all the way from

four to fifteen at various times and in various places, (*four* being the standard number for a long time). These lines (when there were quite a number in the staff) were often divided into *groups of four* by *red* lines, which were not themselves used for notes. These red lines were gradually omitted and the staff divided into sections by a space, as in modern usage. The number of lines in each section was changed to five (in some cases six) for the sake of having a larger available range in each section.

The clefs at the beginning of the staffs are of course simply altered forms of the letters F, C, and G, which were written at first by Guido and others to make the old neume notation more definite.

The staccato sign seems not to have appeared until about the time of Bach, the legato sign being also invented at about the same time. The fermata was first used in imitative part-writing to show where each part was to stop, but with the development of harmonic writing the present practice was inaugurated. Leger lines came into use in the seventeenth century.

Sharps and flats were invented because composers found it necessary to use other tones than those that could be represented by the staff degrees in their natural condition. The history of their origin and development is somewhat complicated and cannot be given here, but it should be noted once more that it was the need of expressing more than could be expressed by the older symbols that called forth the newer and more comprehensive method. The use of sharps and flats in key signatures grew up early in the seventeenth century. In the earlier signatures it was customary to duplicate sharps or flats on staff degrees having the same pitch-name, thus:

(The use of the G clef as here shown did not of course exist at that time.)

The double-sharp and double-flat became necessary when "equal temperament" (making possible the use of the complete cycle of keys) was adopted. This was in the time of Bach (1685–1750).

Signs of expression (relating to tempo and dynamics) date back at least as far as the year 1000 A.D., but the modern terms used for this purpose did not appear until some years after the invention of opera, the date given by C. F. A. Williams in Grove's Dictionary being 1638. These words and signs of expression were at first used only in connection with instrumental music, but were gradually applied to vocal music also.

Other systems of notation have been invented from time to time in the course of the last two or three centuries, but in most cases they have died with their inventors, and in no case has any such system been accepted with anything even approaching unanimity. The tonic-sol-fa system[1] is used quite

---

[1] The *tonic-sol-fa system* represents an attempt to invent a simpler notation to be used by beginners, (especially in the lower grades of the public schools) and by singers in choral societies who have never learned to interpret staff notation and who therefore find some simpler scheme of notation necessary if they are to read music at all.

In this system the syllables *do*, *re*, *mi*, etc., (in phonetic spelling) are used, the tone being arrived at in each case, first by means of a firmly established sense of tonality, and second by associating each diatonic tone with some universally felt emotional feeling: thus *do* is referred to as the *strong* tone, *mi* as the *calm* one, and *la* as the *sad* tone, great emphasis being placed upon *do* as the center of the major tonality, and upon *la* as the center of the minor. The system is thus seen to have one advantage over staff notation, viz.: that in presenting it *the teacher is compelled to begin with a presentation of actual tones*, while in many cases the teacher of staff notation begins by presenting facts regarding the staff and other symbols before the pupil knows anything about tone and rhythm as such.

The symbol for each diatonic tone is the initial letter of the syllable (*i.e.*, d for *do*, r for *re*, etc.), the key being indicated by a letter at the beginning of the composition. The duration-value of tones is indicated by a system of bars, dots, and spaces, the bar being used to indicate the strongest pulse of each measure (as in staff notation) the beats being shown by the mark: a dash indicating the continuation of the same tone through another beat. If a beat has two tones this is indicated by writing the two initial letters representing them with a . between them. A modulation is indicated by giving the new key letter and by printing the syllable-initials from the standpoint of both the old and the new *do*-position. The figure [1] above and to the right of the

extensively in England for vocal music, but has gained little ground anywhere else and the chances are that the present system of notation, with possibly slight additions and modifications, will remain the standard notation for some time to come in spite of the attacks that are periodically made upon it on the ground of cumbersomeness, difficulty in teaching children, etc. The main characteristics of staff notation may be summed up as follows:

1. Pitches represented by lines and spaces of a staff, the higher the line, the higher the pitch represented, signs called clefs at the beginning of each staff making clear the pitch names of the lines and spaces.

2. Duration values shown by *shapes* of notes.

3. Accents shown by position of notes on the staff with regard to bars, *i.e.*, the strongest accent always falls just after the bar, and the beat relatively least accented is found just before the bar.

---

letter indicates the tone in the octave above, while the same figure below and to the right indicates the octave below. A blank space indicates a rest. The tune of My Country, 'Tis of Thee, as printed in tonic sol-fa notation below will make these points clear.

Key F
```
|d  :d  :r  |t, :-.d :r  |m  :m  :f  |m  :-.r :d  |r  :d  :t, |d  :—:— |
|s  :s  :s  |s  :-.f:m  |f  :f  :f  |f  :-.m :r  |m  :f.m:r.d|m  :-.f:s  |
|l.f:m  :r  |d  :—:— |
```

The advantages of the system are (1) the strong sense of key-feeling aroused and the ease with which modulations are felt; and (2) the fact that it is necessary to learn to sing in but one key, thus making sight-singing a much simpler matter, and transposition the easiest process imaginable. But these are advantages from the standpoint of the vocalist (producing but one tone at a time) only, and do not apply to instrumental music. The scheme will therefore probably be always restricted to vocal music and will hardly come into very extensive use even in this field, for the teacher of music is finding it perfectly possible to improve methods of presentation to such an extent that learning to sing from the staff becomes a very simple matter even to the young child. And even though this were not true, the tonic-sol-fa will always be hampered by the fact that since all letters are printed in a straight horizontal line the ear does not have the assistance of the eye in appreciating the rise and fall of melody, as is the case in staff notation.

4. Extent and description of beat-groups shown by measure-signs.

5. Key shown by key signature placed at the beginning of each staff.

6. Rate of speed, dynamic changes, etc., shown by certain Italian words (*allegro*, *andante*, etc.), whose meaning is as universally understood as staff notation itself.

APPENDIX B

Musical Instruments

1. Broadly speaking, musical instruments may be divided into two classes, viz.: (1) those that have a keyboard and are therefore capable of sounding several tones simultaneously; (2) those that (as a rule) sound only one tone at a time, as the violin and trumpet. The piano is of course the most familiar example of the first class, and a brief description is therefore given.

The *piano* was invented about two hundred years ago by Cristofori (1651–1731), an Italian. It was an enormous improvement over the types of key-board instrument that were in use at that time (clavichord, harpsichord, spinet, virginal) and has resulted in an entirely different style of composition. See note on embellishments, p. 26.

2. The most characteristic things about the *piano* as contrasted with its immediate predecessors are : (1) that on it the loudness and softness of the tone can be regulated by the force with which the keys are struck (hence the name *piano-forte* meaning literally the *soft-loud*); (2) the fact that the piano is capable of sustaining tone to a much greater extent than its predecessors. In other words the tone continues sounding for some little time after the key is struck, while on the earlier instruments it stopped almost instantly after being sounded.

The essentials of the piano mechanism are:

1. Felt hammers controlled by keys, each hammer striking two or three strings (which are tuned in unison) and immediately rebounding from these strings, allowing them to vibrate as long as the key

is held down. The mechanism that allows the hammers to rebound from the strings and fall into position for another blow is called the *escapement*.

2. A damper (made of softer felt) pressing against each string and preventing it from vibrating until it is wanted.

3. A keyboard action that controls both hammers and dampers, causing the damper to leave the string at the same instant that the hammer strikes it.

4. A pedal (damper pedal) controlling all of the dampers, so that at any moment all the strings may be released so as to be free to vibrate.

Other interesting details are:

1. The strings are stretched over a thin sheet of wood called the sound-board. This aids greatly in intensifying the tone.

2. The soft pedal (the one at the left) in an *upright piano* causes the hammers to move up nearer the strings, and the shorter swing thus afforded causes a less violent blow and consequently a softer tone. In the *grand piano* this same pedal shifts the mechanism to one side so that the hammers strike only one or two of the strings, this resulting in a softer tone of somewhat modified quality.

These details regarding the mechanism of the piano can easily be verified by removing the front of any ordinary upright piano and observing what takes place when the keys are struck or the pedals depressed.

3. There are two familiar types of *organ* in use at the present time, (1) the reed organ, (2) the pipe-organ.

The *reed organ* is very simple in construction, the tone being produced by the vibration of metal reeds (fixed in little cells), through which air is forced (or sucked) from the bellows, the latter being usually worked by the feet of the player.

More power may be secured either by drawing additional stops, thus throwing on more sets of reeds, or by opening the knee swells which either throw on more reeds (sometimes octave couplers) or else open a *swell box* in which some of the reeds are enclosed, the tone being louder when the box is open than when closed. More tone may also be secured by pumping harder.

4. The essential characteristic of the *pipe-organ* is a number of sets or registers of pipes called *stops*, each set being capable (usually) of sounding the entire chromatic scale through a range of five or six octaves. Thus for example when the stop *melodia* is drawn (by pulling out a stop-knob or tilting a tablet), one set of pipes only, sounds when the keyboard is played on: but if the stop *flute* is drawn with *melodia*, two pipes speak every time a key is depressed. Thus if an organ has forty *speaking stops*, all running through the entire keyboard, then each time one key is depressed forty pipes will speak, and if a chord of five tones is played, two hundred pipes will speak.   The object of having so many pipes is not merely to make possible a very powerful tone, but, rather, to give greater variety of tone-color.

The pipe-organ usually has a pedal keyboard on which the feet of the performer play a bass part, this part often sounding an octave (or more) lower than the notes indicate.

An *eight-foot stop* on the organ produces tones of the same pitches as the piano when corresponding keys are struck: A *four-foot stop* sounds tones an octave higher and a *two-foot stop* tones two octaves higher. A *sixteen-foot stop* sounds tones an octave lower than the piano, and a *thirty-two foot* stop, tones two octaves lower, while some organs have also a *sixty-four foot* stop which sounds three octaves lower.   This gives the organ an exceedingly wide range, its compass being greater than that of any other single instrument, and comparable in both range of pitches and variety of color only with the modern orchestra.

Modern pipe-organs always have a number of *combination pedals* or *pistons* (usually both), by means of which the organist is enabled to throw on a number of stops with one movement. The selection and use of suitable stops, couplers, combinations, etc., is called *registration*.

5. The instruments mentioned at the beginning of this appendix as belonging to the second class are more familiar in connection with ensemble playing, being commonly associated with either band or orchestra.

6. A *band* is a company of musicians all of whom play upon either wind or percussion instruments, the main body of tone being produced by the brass and wood-wind divisions.

Sousa's band is usually made up in somewhat the following manner: 4 flutes and piccolos, 12 B♭ clarinets, 1 E♭ clarinet, 1 alto clarinet, 1 bass clarinet, 2 oboes, 2 bassoons, 2 sarrusophones, 4 saxophones, 4 cornets, 2 trumpets, 1 soprano saxhorn (fluegelhorn), 4 French horns, 4 trombones, 2 contrabass tubas, 4 tubas, 1 snare drum, 1 bass drum, 2 kettle drums, cymbals, triangle, bells, castanets, xylophone, etc.

7. An *orchestra* is a company of musicians performing upon stringed instruments as well as upon wind and percussion. It is differentiated from the band by the fact that the main body of tone is produced by the strings.

There are *four classes of instruments* in the orchestra, viz., *strings, wood-wind, brass (wind)* and *percussion.* In addition to these four classes, there is the *harp,* which although a stringed instrument, does not belong in the same group as the other strings because the manner of producing the tone is altogether different.

8. In the first group (the *strings*) are found the first and second violins, viola, violoncello (usually spelled *cello*), and double-bass. The first and second violins are identical in every way (but play different parts), while the other members of the family merely represent larger examples of the same type of instrument.

9. In the second group (the *wood-wind*) are found the flute, piccolo, oboe, bassoon, English horn, double-bassoon,

clarinet, and bass clarinet.   The English horn, double-bassoon, bass clarinet, and piccolo are not called for in the older compositions, hence are not always present in the orchestra.

10. In the third group (the *brass choir*) are found the French horn, (usually referred to as *the horn*), trumpet (sometimes replaced by the cornet) trombone, and tuba.

11. The fourth group (*percussion*) consists of kettle drums, bass drum, cymbals, snare drum, triangle, bells, etc.

12. In an orchestra of about 100 players the proportion of instruments is as about as follows, although it varies somewhat according to the taste of the conductor, the style of composition to be performed, etc.:

18 first violins, 16 second violins, 14 violas, 12 cellos, 10 basses, 1 harp, 3 flutes, 1 piccolo, 3 oboes, 1 English horn, 3 clarinets, 1 bass clarinet, 3 bassoons, 1 contra (or double) bassoon, 4 horns, 2 trumpets, 3 trombones, 1 tuba, 3 kettle drums, 1 bass drum, 1 snare drum, 1 each of triangle, cymbals, bells, and other instruments of percussion, several of which are often manipulated by one performer.

13. The cuts and brief descriptions here added will give at least a rudimentary idea of the appearance and possibilities of the instruments most commonly used in bands and orchestras.   For fuller descriptions and particulars regarding range, quality, etc., the student is referred to Mason's "The Orchestral Instruments and What They Do," Lavignac's "Music and Musicians," and to the various articles which describe each instrument under its own name in Grove's Dictionary or in any good encyclopaedia.   For still fuller details some work on orchestration will have to be consulted.

14. The *violin* has four strings, tuned thus , these making available a range of about three and one-half octaves $(g - c'''')$.   This range[1] may be extended upward somewhat

---

[1] The ranges noted in connection with these descriptions of instruments are ordinarily the *practical orchestral or band* ranges rather than those which are possible in solo performance.

further by means of *harmonics*, these being produced by lightly touching the string at certain points (while the bow is moving across it) instead of holding it down against the finger-board. The highest string of the *violin* (viola and cello also) is often called the *chanterelle* because it is most often used for playing the melody. The *violin* ordinarily produces but one tone at a time, but by *stopping* two strings simultaneously and so drawing the bow as to set both in vibration, two tones may be produced at the same time, while three and four tones can be sounded *almost* simultaneously.

VIOLIN.
Length, 23½ inches.
Length of bow, 29½ inches.

The *mute* (or *sordino*) is a small clamp made of metal, wood, or ivory, which when clipped to the top of the bridge causes the vibrations to be transmitted less freely to the body of the violin, giving rise to a tone modified in quality, and decreased in power.

For certain special effects the player is directed to pluck the string (*pizzicato*), this method of playing giving rise to a dry, detached tone instead of the smooth, flowing one that is so characteristic of the *violin* as commonly played.

Violins in the orchestra are divided into firsts and seconds, the *first violins* being always seated at the left of the audience and the *seconds* at the right.

VIOLA.
Length, 26 in. Length of bow, 28.

15. The *viola* has four strings, also tuned in fifths, thus the violin at a little larger sized violin, Its tone is not so in-

The *viola* looks exactly like distance, and is really only a having a range a fifth lower. cisive as that of the violin, being rather heavier — "more gloomy," as it is often described. The *viola* is not so useful as the violin as a solo instrument because it is not capable of producing so many varities of color, nevertheless it is invaluable for certain effects. In orchestral music it is of course one of the most valuable instruments for filling in the harmony. The *viola* players are usually seated behind the second violin players in the orchestra.

16. The *violoncello* or *cello* (sometimes called *bass viol*) has four strings, tuned thus: Its range is about three and one-half octaves (from C to e″ or f″), but in solo work this range is sometimes extended much higher. The *cello* is much more universally used as a solo instrument than the viola and its tone is capable of a much greater degree of variation. In the orchestra it plays the bass of the string quartet (reinforced by the double-bass), but is also often used for solo passages. *Con sordino* and *pizzicato* passages occur as often for the *cello* as for the violin.

VIOLONCELLO.
Length, 3 ft. 10 in.
Length of bow, 28 in.

17. The *double bass* differs from the other members of the string family in that it is tuned in *fourths* instead of in *fifths*. Its four strings are tuned as follows the entire range of the instrument being from EE to a. In music written for double-bass the notes are always printed an octave higher than the tones are to sound: that is, when the bass-player sees the note he plays this being done to avoid leger lines. The tone of the *bass* is much heavier and

the instrument itself is much more clumsy to handle than the other members of the group, hence it is almost never used as a solo instrument but it is invaluable for reinforcing the bass part in orchestral music. The mute is rarely used on the *double-bass*, but the *pizzicato* effect is very common and the bass pizzicato tone is much fuller and richer than that of any other stringed instrument.

18. The *flute* has a range of three octaves.

It is used in both solo and orchestral playing as well as in bands. The flute was formerly always made of wood, but is at present often made of metal.

19. The *piccolo* is a flute playing an octave higher than the one described above. The notes are printed as for the flute, but the player understands that the tone is to sound an octave higher. The *piccolo* is used widely in

DOUBLE-BASS.
Length, 6 ft. 6 in. Length of bow, 23½ in.

band music and quite often in orchestral music also, but since the tone is so brilliant and penetrating and is incapable of any great variation, it is not suitable for solo performance.

Range

OBOE.
(hautboy.)
Length,
24½ in.

CONTRA BASSOON.
(Double bassoon.)

Length 6 ft. Range
about an octave lower
than bassoon, but not
all tones in this range
are practicable.

Range

ENGLISH
HORN.
(Cor.
Anglais)
Length, 2 ft.
11½ in.

PICCOLO.

Length, 13 in.
(Note that this
is approxi-
mately half the
length of the
flute.)

FLUTE.
Length,
26¼ in.

Range

BASSOON.
(fagotto.)
Length, 4 ft. 3½ in.

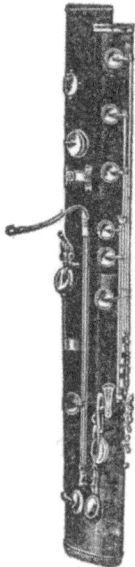

20. The next four instruments to be described (*oboe, bassoon, English horn,* and *contra bassoon*) are often referred to as the *oboe family* since the principle of tone production and general manipulation is the same in all four. The tone in these instruments is produced by the vibration of two very thin pieces of cane, which are called together a *double-reed.*

The *oboe* is especially valuable in the orchestra as a solo instrument, and its thin, nasal tones are suggestive of rustic, pastoral simplicity, both *oboe* and *English horn* being often used by orchestral composers in passages intended to express the idea of rural out-of-door life. The *English horn* is also often used in passages where the idea of melancholy and suffering is to be conveyed to the audience. In a military band the oboe corresponds to the first violin of the orchestra.

The *bassoon* and *contra-bassoon* are used mostly to provide a bass part for the harmony of the wood-wind group, but they are also sometimes employed (especially the *bassoon*) to depict comic or grotsesque effects.

21. The next two types of instruments to be described (*clarinet* and *saxophone*) are alike in that the tone is produced by the vibration of a *single* strip of cane (called *single reed*) which is held against the lower lip of the player. The *clarinet* and *bass clarinet* are made of wood and are used in both bands and orchestras, but the *saxophone* is usually made of metal, and, the tone being more

BASS CLARINET.
Length, 3 ft. 3 in.
Range

CLARINET.
Length, 28 in.

strident and penetrating, the instrument is ordinarily used only in combination with other wind instruments, *i.e.*, in bands.

Since the fingering of the *clarinet* is excessively difficult the performer can play in only certain keys on the same instrument, hence to play in different keys *clarinets* in several keys must be provided, there being usually three in all. The music is written as though it were to be played in the key of C, but the tones produced are actually in other keys. For this reason the *clarinet* is called a *transposing instrument*. The range of the *clarinet* is the greatest possessed by any of the wind instruments, that of the clarinet in C being from

to

SAXOPHONES.

SOPRANO.   ALTO.   TENOR.   BASS.
Length, 15⅜ in.   Length, 2 ft. 7½ in.   Length, 3 ft. 9 in.
Combined range

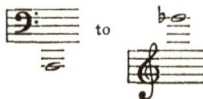 to

The *sarrusophone* is an instrument with a double-reed. It is made of brass and exists in several sizes, the only one ever used in the orchestra being the double-bass *sarrusophone*, which has approximately the same range as the double-bassoon and is sometimes (but rarely) made use of in the orchestra instead of the latter instrument. The tone of the *sarrusophone* is something like that of the bassoon.

22. The *French horn* (often called *valve horn* or simply *horn*) really consists of a long tube (about 16 feet) which is bent into circular form for convenience in handling. Its range is from 𝄢 to 𝄞. In the orchestra *French horns* are used in pairs,

FRENCH HORN. Length, 22⅜ in.

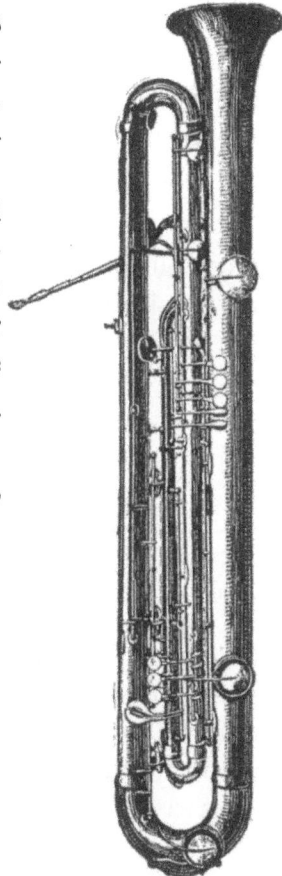

SARRUSOPHONE.

two of the players taking the higher tones, and two the lower. The tone is intensely mellow but incapable of any extensive variation, but in spite of this lack of variety the tone itself is so wonderfully beautiful that the instrument is one of the most useful in the orchestra both in solo passages and to fill in the harmony. The *horn* (as well as the trumpet and trombone) differs from most of the wood-wind instruments in that its mouthpiece contains no reed, the lips of the player constituting the vibrating body as they are stretched across the mouthpiece and air is forced against them. The *horn* is used in bands as well as in orchestras.

23. The range of the *trumpet* is [music notation], the typical tone being brilliant and ringing. It is used in both band and orchestra, playing the highest parts assigned to the brass choir.

TRUMPET. Length, 22½ in.

The *trumpet* is often replaced in both band and orchestra by its less refined cousin the *cornet* because of the ease with which the latter can be played as compared with the trumpet, and the larger number of players that are available in consequence of this ease of execution.

24. The *cornet* looks something like the trumpet, but is not so slim and graceful in appearance. Its tube is only four and one-half feet long, as compared with a length of about eight feet in the trumpet, and sixteen feet in the French horn.

The range of the *cornet* in B♭ is from [music notation] to [music notation].

The tone is somewhat commonplace as compared with the

trumpet, but because of its great agility in the rendition of trills, repeated tones, etc., it is universally used in all sorts of combinations, even (as noted above) taking the place of the trumpet in many small orchestras.

25. The pitch sounded by the *trombone* is altered by lengthening or shortening the tube of which the instrument is constructed, this being possible because the lower part slides into the upper and can be pulled out to increase the total length of the tube through which the air passes. There are usually three *trombones* in the orchestra, each playing a separate part, and the combination of this trio with the *tuba* re-inforcing the bass parts is majestic and thrilling, being powerful enough to dominate the entire orchestra in *Fortissimo* passages. But the *trombones* are useful in soft passages also, and their tone when playing pianissimo is rich, serene, and sonorous.

CORNET.
Length, 13¾ in.

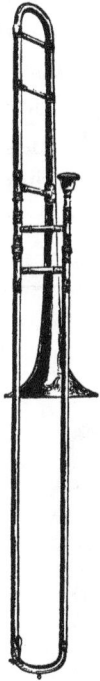

SLIDE TROMBONE. Length, 3 ft. 9 in.

Range of tenor trombone (the size ordinarily used)

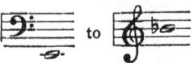

26. The *bass tuba* is a member of the saxhorn family[1] and

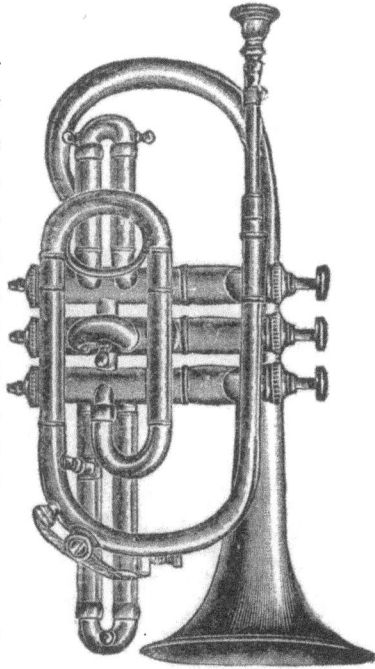

---

[1] The *sax-horn* was invented about 1840 by Adolphe Sax, a Frenchman. The *saxophone* is the invention of the same man.

supplies the lowest part of the brass choir, as the double-bass does in the string choir.   It is used in both orchestra and band, being often supported in the larger bands by a still lower-toned member of the same family — the *contra-bass tuba*. The range of the *tuba* is from

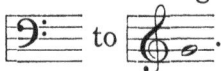

$$\text{[musical staff]} \text{ to } \text{[musical staff]}.$$

27. The *kettle-drum* is the most important member of the percussion family and is always used either in pairs or in threes. The size of these instruments varies somewhat with the make, but when two drums are used the diameter is approximately that given under

BASS TUBA.   Length, 3 ft. 3 in.

the illustration.   The range of a pair of *drums* is *one octave* [musical staff]

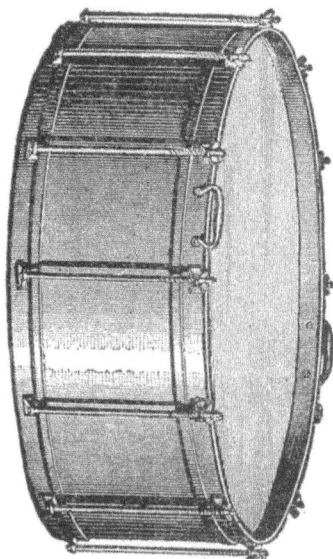

BASS DRUM.   Diameter about 2½ ft.   CYMBALS.   Diameter, 13½ in.

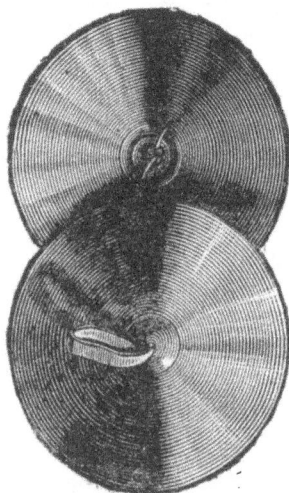

and when but two drums are used the larger one takes the tones from F to about C of this range, and the smaller takes those

from about B♭ to F.   The most common usage is to tune one
drum to the *tonic*, and the other to the *dominant* of the key in

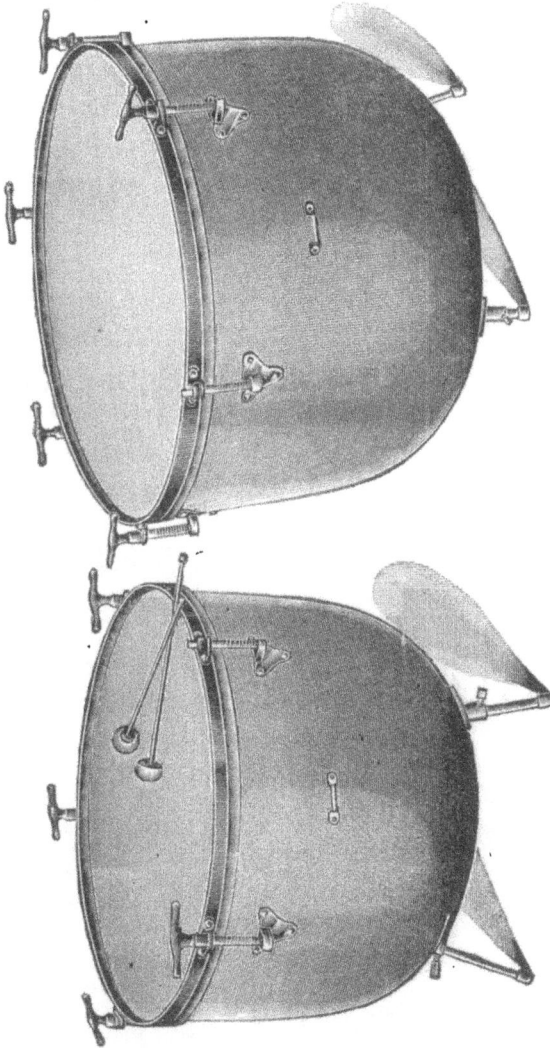

KETTLE-DRUMS.   Diameter of head, 24¾ in. and 27½ ins.

which the composition is written.   The pitch of the *kettle-*
drum can be varied by increasing or lessening the tension of
the head by means of thumb-screws which act on a metal
ring.

The other important members of the percussion family are shown on this and the following page, their use being so obvious as to require no detailed explanation.

TAMBOURINE.
Diameter, 10 to 12 in.

BELLS.
(Fr. carillon ; Ger. Glockenspiel.)

SIDE DRUM. Diameter, about 15½ in.

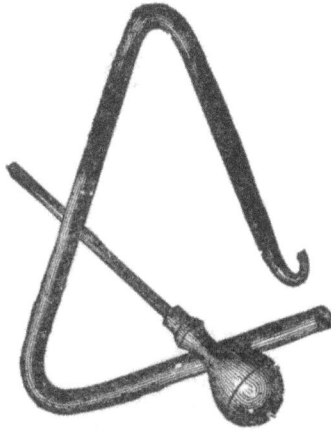

TRIANGLE. Height, about 8 in.

28. The *harp* is one of the oldest of instruments (dating back over 6000 years), but it is only in comparatively recent years that it has been used in the symphony orchestra. Its range is from $\begin{array}{c}\text{\large 9:}\end{array}$ to $\begin{array}{c}\text{\large #}\end{array}$.

The modern *double-action harp* has forty-six strings, which are tuned in half-steps and whole-steps so as to sound the scale of C♭ major. It has a series of seven pedals around its base, each pedal having two *notches* below it, into either of which the pedal may be lowered and held fast. The first pedal shortens the F♭ string so that it now sounds F, (giving the key of G♭); the second one

HARP. Height, 5 ft. 8 in.

shortens the C♭ string so that it sounds C (giving the key of D♭); the third pedal shortens the G♭ string so that it sounds G (giving the key of A♭); the fourth changes D♮ to D (giving the key of E♭), and so on until, when all the pedals are fixed in their first notches, the scale of C is sounded instead of C♭ as was the case before any of the pedals were depressed. But if the first pedal is now pushed down into the second notch the original F♭ string is still further shortened and now sounds the pitch F♯ (giving us the key of G), and if all the other pedals are likewise successively lowered to the second notch we get in turn all the *sharp keys* — D, A, E, B, F♯ and C♯, the last-named key being obtained as the result of having all the pedals fixed in their second notches, thus making all the tones of the original C♭ scale a whole-step higher so that they now sound the C♯ scale.

Chords of not more than four tones for each hand may be played simultaneously on the harp, but arpeggio and scale passages are the rule, and are more successful than simultaneous chords. The notation of harp music is essentially like that of piano music.

APPENDIX C

ACOUSTICS

NOTE: — It is usually taken for granted that the student of music is familiar with the significance of such terms as *over-tone, equal temperament,* etc., and with principles such as that relating to the relation between vibration rates and pitches: the writer has in his own experience found, however, that most students are not at all familiar with such data, and this appendix is therefore added in the hope that a few facts at least regarding the laws of sound may be brought to the attention of some who would otherwise remain in entire ignorance of the subject.

1. *Acoustics* is the science which deals with sound and the laws of its production and transmission. Since all sound is caused by vibration, *acoustics* may be defined as the science which treats of the phenomena of sound-producing vibration.

2. All sound (as stated above) is produced by vibration of some sort: strike a tuning-fork against the top of a table and *see* the vibrations which cause the tone, or, if the fork is a small one and the vibrations cannot be seen, hold it against the edge of a sheet of paper and hear the blows it strikes; or, watch one of the lowest strings of the piano after striking the key a sharp blow; or, look closely at the heavier strings of the violin (or better still, the cello) and watch them oscillate rapidly to and fro as the bow moves across them.

The vibrating body may be a string, a thin piece of wood, a piece of metal, a membrane (cf. drum), the lips (cf. playing the cornet), the vocal cords, etc. Often it is a column of air whose vibrations give rise to the tone, the reed or other medium merely serving to set the air in vibration.

3. Sound is *transmitted* through the air in somewhat this fashion: the vibrating body (a string for example) strikes the air-particles in its immediate vicinity, and they, being in con-

tact with other such air-particles, strike these others, the latter
in turn striking yet others, and so on, both a forward and backward movement being set up (oscillation). These particles
lie so close together that no movement at all can be detected,
and it is only when the disturbance finally reaches the air-
particles that are in contact with the ear-drum that any effect
is evident.

This phenomenon of sound-transmission may perhaps be
made more clear by the old illustration of a series of eight
billiard balls in a row on a table: if the first ball is tapped
lightly, striking gently against ball number 2, the latter (as
well as numbers 3, 4, 5, 6, and 7) will not apparently move at
all, but ball number 8 at the other end will roll away. The
air-particles act upon each other in much this same fashion,
the difference being that when they are set in motion by a
vibrating body a complete vibration backward and forward
causes a similar *backward and forward* movement of the particles (oscillation) instead of simply a *forward jerk* as in the
case of the billiard balls.

Another way of describing the same process is this: the
vibration of some body produces waves in the air (cf. waves
in the ocean, which carry water forward but do not themselves
move on continuously), these waves spread out spherically
(i.e. in all directions) and finally reach the ear, where they set
the ear-drum in vibration, thus sending certain sound-stimuli
to the nerves of hearing in the inner ear, and thus to the brain.

An important thing to be noted in connection with sound-
transmission is that sound will not travel in a vacuum: some
kind of a medium is essential for its transmission. This
medium may be air, water, a bar of iron or steel, the earth, etc.

4. The *rate* at which sound travels through the air is
about 1100 feet per second, the rapidity varying somewhat
with fluctuations in temperature and humidity. In water the
rate is much higher than in air (about four times as great)

while the velocity of sound through other mediums (as *e.g.*, steel) is sometimes as much as sixteen times as great as through air.

5. Sound, like light, may be *intensified* by a suitable reflecting surface directly back of the vibrating body (cf. sounding board); it may also be reflected by some surface at a distance from its source in such a way that at a certain point (the focus) the sound may be very clearly heard, but at other places, even those *nearer* the source of sound, it can scarcely be heard at all. If there is such a surface in an auditorium (as often occurs) there will be a certain point where everything can be heard very easily, but in the rest of the room it may be very difficult to understand what is being said or sung.

Echoes are caused by sound-reflection, the distance of the reflecting surface from the vibrating body determining the number of syllables that will be echoed.

The *acoustics* of an auditorium (*i.e.*, its hearing properties) depend upon the position and nature of the reflecting surfaces and also upon the length of time a sound persists after the vibrating body has stopped. If it persists longer than $2\frac{1}{4}$ or $2\frac{1}{3}$ seconds the room will not be suitable for musical performances because of the mixture of persisting tones with following ones, this causing a blurred effect somewhat like that obtained by playing a series of unrelated chords on the piano while the damper-pedal is held down. The duration of the reverberation depends upon the size and height of the room, material of floor and walls, furniture, size of audience, etc.

6. Sound may be classified roughly into *tones* and *noises* although the line of cleavage is not always sharply drawn. If I throw stones at the side of a barn, sounds are produced, but they are caused by irregular vibrations of an irregularly constructed surface and are referred to as *noise*. But if I tap the head of a kettle-drum, a regular series of vibrations is set up and the resulting sound is referred to as *tone*. In general the

material of music consists of tones, but for special effects certain noises are also utilized (cf. castanets, etc.).

7. Musical tones have three properties, viz.:

        1. Pitch.

        2. Intensity.

        3. Quality (timbre).

By *pitch* is meant the highness or lowness of tone. It depends upon rate of vibration. If a body vibrates only 8 or 10 times per second no tone is heard at all: but if it vibrates regularly at the rate of 16 or 18 per second a tone of very low pitch is heard. If it vibrates at the rate of 24 the pitch is higher, at 30 higher still, at 200 yet higher, and when a rate of about 38,000 per second has been reached the pitch is so high that most ears cannot perceive it at all. The highest tone that can ordinarily be heard is the E♭ four octaves higher than the highest E♭ of the piano. The entire range of sound humanly audible is therefore about eleven octaves (rates 16–38,000), but only about *eight* of these octaves are utilized for musical purposes. The tones of the piano (with a range of 7⅓ octaves) are produced by vibration rates approximately between 27 and 4224. In the orchestra the range is slightly more extended, the rates being from 33 to 4752.

Certain interesting facts regarding the relation between vibration-rates and pitches have been worked out: it has been discovered for instance that if the number of vibrations is doubled, the pitch of the resulting tone is an octave higher; *i.e.*, if a string vibrating at the rate of 261 per second gives rise to the pitch c′, then a string one-half as long and vibrating twice as rapidly (522) will give rise to the pitch c″, *i.e.*, an octave higher than c′. In the same way it has been found that if the rate is multiplied by ⁵⁄₄ the pitch of the tone will be a *major third* higher; if multiplied by ⅗, a *perfect fifth* higher, etc. These laws are often stated thus: the ratio of the octave to the fundamental is as two is to one; that of the major third as five is to four; that of the perfect fifth as three is to two, and so on through the entire series of pitches embraced within the octave, the *ratio* being of course the same for all octaves.

9. The *intensity* (loudness or softness) of tones depends upon the amplitude (width) of the vibrations, a louder tone being the result of vibrations of greater amplitude, and vice versa. This may be verified by plucking a long string (on cello or double-bass) and noting that when plucked gently vibrations of small amplitude are set up, while a vigorous pluck results in much wider vibrations, and, consequently, in a louder tone. It should be noted that the *pitch* of the tone is not affected by the change in amplitude of vibration.

The intensity of tones varies with the medium conveying them, being usually louder at night because the air is then more elastic. Tone intensity is also affected by *sympathetic vibrations* set up in other bodies. If two strings of the same length are stretched side by side and one set in vibration so as to produce tone the other will soon begin to vibrate also and the combined tone will be louder than if only one string produced it. This phenomenon is the basis of what is known as resonance (cf. body of violin, resonance cavities of nose and mouth, sounding board of piano, etc.).

10. *Quality* depends upon the shape (or form) of the vibrations which give rise to the tone. A series of simple vibrations will cause a simple (or colorless) tone, while complex vibrations (giving rise to overtones of various kinds and in a variety of proportions) cause more individualistic peculiarities of quality. Quality is affected also by the shape and size of the resonance body. (Cf. last part of sec. 9 above.)

11. Practically every musical tone really consists of a combination of several tones sounding simultaneously, the combined effect upon the ear giving the impression of a single tone. The most important tone of the series is the *fundamental,* which dominates the combination and gives the pitch,

but this fundamental is practically always combined with a greater or less number of faint and elusive attending tones called *overtones* or *harmonics*. The first of these overtones is the octave above the fundamental; the second is the fifth above this octave; the third, two octaves above the fundamental, and so on through the series as shown in the figure below. The presence of these *overtones* is accounted for by the fact that the string (or other vibrating body) does not merely vibrate in its entirety but has in addition to the principal oscillation a number of sectional movements also. Thus it is easily proved that a string vibrates in halves, thirds, etc., in addition to the principal vibration of the entire string, and it is the vibration of these halves, thirds, etc., which gives rise to the *harmonics*, or *upper partials* as they are often called. The figure shows *Great C* and its first eight overtones. A similar series might be worked out from any other fundamental.

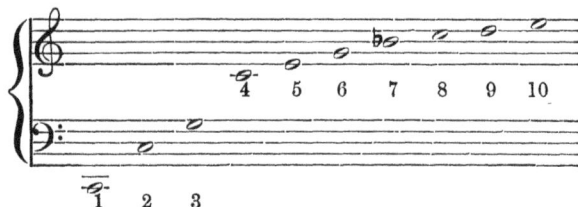

(NOTE: — The B♭ in this series is approximate only.)

It will be recalled that in the section (10) dealing with *quality* the statement was made that *quality* depends upon the shape of the vibrations; it should now be noted that it is the form of these vibrations that determines the nature and proportion of the overtones and hence the quality. Thus *e.g.*, a tone that has too large a proportion of the fourth upper partial (*i.e.*, the *third* of the chord) will be *reedy* and somewhat unpleasant. This is the case with many voices that are referred to as *nasal*. Too great a proportion of overtones is what causes certain pianos to sound "tin-panny." The tone pro-

duced by a good tuning-fork is almost entirely free from overtones: it has therefore no distinctive quality and is said to be
a *simple* tone. The characteristic tone of the oboe on the
other hand has many overtones and is therefore highly individualistic: this enables us to recognize the tone of the instrument even though we cannot see the player. Such a tone
is said to be *complex*.

12. The mathematical ratio referred to on page 134, if
strictly carried out in tuning a keyboard instrument would
cause the half-steps to vary slightly in size, and playing in
certain keys (especially those having a number of sharps or
flats in the signature) would therefore sound out of tune.
There would be many other disadvantages in such a system,
notably the inability to modulate freely to other keys, and
since modulation is one of the predominant and most striking
characteristics of modern music, this would constitute a serious
barrier to advances in composition. To obviate these disadvantages a system of *equal temperament* was invented and has
been in universal use since the time of Bach (1685–1750) who
was the first prominent composer to use it extensively. *Equal
temperament* means simply dividing the octave into twelve
equal parts, thus causing all scales (as played on keyboard
instruments at least) to sound exactly alike.

To show the practicability of equal temperament Bach wrote a series of 48 *preludes
and fugues*, two in each major and two in each minor key. He called the collection
"The Well-tempered Clavichord."

13. Various *standards of pitch* have existed at different
times in the last two centuries, and even now there is no absolute uniformity although conditions are much better than
they were even twenty-five years ago. Scientists use what is
known as the "scientific standard" (sometimes called the
"philosophic standard"), viz., 256 double vibrations for
"middle C." This pitch is not in actual use for musical purposes, but is retained for theoretical purposes because of its

convenience of computation (being a power of 2). In 1885 a conference of musicians at Vienna ratified the pitch giving "middle C 261 vibrations, this having been adopted by the French as their official pitch some 26 years before. In 1891 a convention of piano manufacturers at Philadelphia adopted this same pitch for the United States, and it has been in practically universal use ever since. This pitch (giving Middle C 261 vibrations) is known as "International Pitch."

Concert pitch is slightly higher than International, the difference between the two varying somewhat, but being almost always less than one-half step. This higher pitch is still often used by bands and sometimes by orchestras to give greater brilliancy to the wind instruments.

REFERENCES

Lavignac — Music and Musicians, pp. 1–66.
Broadhouse — The Student's Helmholz.
Helmholtz — Sensations of Tone.
Hamilton — Sound and its Relation to Music.
NOTE: — For a simple and illuminating treatment of the subject from the standpoint of the music student, the books by Lavignac and Hamilton are especially recommended.

APPENDIX D

Terminology Reform

A recent writer[1] on *vocal terminology* makes the following statement as an introduction to certain remarks advocating a more definite use of terms relating to tone production by the human voice: — "The correct use of words is the most potent factor in the development of the thinker." If this statement has any basis of fact whatsoever to support it then it must be evident to the merest novice in musical work that the popular use of many common terms by musicians is keeping a good many people from clear and logical thought in a field that needs accurate thinkers very badly! However this may be, it must be patent to all that our present terminology is in many respects neither correct nor logical, and the movement inaugurated by the Music Section of the National Education Association some years ago to secure greater uniformity in the use and definition of certain expressions should therefore not only command the respect and commendation, but the active support of all progressive teachers of music.

Let it be noted at the outset that such reforms as are advocated by the committee will never come into general use while the rank and file of teachers throughout the country merely *approve* the reports so carefully compiled and submitted each year: these reforms will become effective only as individual teachers make up their minds that the end to be attained is worth the trouble of being careful to use only correct

---

[1] Floyd S. Muckey — "Vocal Terminology," *The Musician*, May, 1912, p. 337.

terminology every day for a month, or three months, or a year — whatever length of time may be necessary in order to get the new habits fixed in mind and muscle.

The Terminology Committee was appointed by the Department of Music of the N. E. A. in 1906 and made its first report at Los Angeles in 1907. Since then the indefatigable chairman of the committee (Mr. Chas. I. Rice, of Worcester, Mass.) has contributed generously of both time and strength, and has by his annual reports to the Department set many of us to thinking along certain new lines, and has caused some of us at any rate to adopt in our own teaching certain changes of terminology which have enabled us to make our work more effective.

In his first report Mr. Rice says:

"Any one who has observed the teaching of school music in any considerable number of places in this country cannot fail to have remarked the great diversity of statement employed by different teachers regarding the facts which we are engaged in teaching, and the equal diversity of terminology used in teaching the symbols by which musicians seek to record these facts. To the teacher of exact sciences our picturesque use of the same term to describe two or more entirely different things never ceases to be a marvel. . . . Thoughtful men and women will become impressed with the untruthfulness of certain statements and little by little change their practice. Others will follow, influenced by example. The revolutionists will deride us for not moving faster while the conservatives will be suspicious of any change."

At this meeting in Los Angeles a list of thirteen points was recommended by the committee and adopted by the Music Department. These points are given in the N. E. A. Volume of Proceedings for 1907, p. 875.

Since 1907 the committee (consisting· of Chas. I. Rice, P. C. Hayden, W. B. Kinnear, Leo R. Lewis, and Constance

Barlow-Smith) have each year selected a number of topics for discussion, and have submitted valuable reports recommending the adoption of certain reforms. Some of the points recommended have usually been rejected by the Department, but many of them have been adopted and the reports of the committee have set many teachers thinking and have made us all more careful in the use and definition of common terms. A complete list of all points adopted by the Department since 1907 has been made by Mr. Rice for *School Music*, and this list is here reprinted from the January, 1913, number of that magazine.

TERMINOLOGY ADOPTIONS, 1907–1910

1. *Tone:* Specific name for a musical sound of definite pitch. Use neither *sound*, a general term, nor *note*, a term of notation.

2. *Interval:* The pitch relation between *two* tones. Not properly applicable to a single tone or scale degree. Example: "Sing the fifth tone of the scale." Not "sing the fifth interval of the scale."

3. *Key:* Tones in relation to a tonic. Example: In the key of G. *Not* in the scale of G. Scales, major and minor are composed of a definite selection from the many tones of the key, and all scales extend through at least one octave of pitch. The chromatic scale utilizes all the tones of a key within the octave.

4. *Natural:* Not a suitable compound to use in naming pitches. Pitch names are either *simple:* B, or *compound:* B sharp, B double-sharp, B flat or B double-flat, and there is no pitch named "B natural." Example: Pitch B, *not* "B natural."

NOTE: — L. R. L. thinks that B natural should be the name when the notation suggests it.

5. *Step, Half-step:* Terms of interval *measurement.* Avoid *tone, semi-tone* or *half-tone.* Major second and minor second are interval names. Example: How large are the following intervals? (1) Major second, (2) minor second, (3) augmented prime. Answer: (1) a step, (2) a half-step, (3) a half-step.

6. *Chromatic:* A tone of the key which is not a member of its diatonic scale. (N. B.) An accidental (a notation sign) is not a chromatic sign *unless* it makes a staff-degree represent a chromatic tone.

7. *Major; Minor:* Major and Minor keys having the same signature should be called relative major and minor. Major and minor keys having the same tonic, but different signatures, should be called tonic major and minor. Not "parallel" major or minor in either case.

8. *Staff:* Five horizontal lines and their spaces. Staff *lines* are named (numbered) upward in order, first to fifth. *Spaces:* Space below, first-second-third-fourth-space, and space above[1]. (Six in all.) Additional short lines and their short spaces numbered outward both ways from the main staff, viz: line below, second space below. The boundary of the staff is always a space.

9. *G Clef, F Clef, C Clef:* These clefs when placed upon the staff, give its degrees their first, or primary pitch meaning. Each makes the degree it occupies represent a pitch of its respective name. Example: The G clef makes the second line represent the pitch G. Avoid "*fixes G on.*" The staff with clef in position represents only pitches having *simple* or *one-word* names, A, B, C, etc.

10. *Sharps, Flats:* Given a staff with clef in position as in example above, sharps and flats make staff degrees upon which they are placed represent pitches a half-step higher or lower. These pitches have compound or two-word names. Example: The second line stands for the pitch G (simple name). Sharp the second line and it will stand for the pitch G sharp. (Compound name.) The third line stands for the pitch B. (Simple name.) Flat it, and the line will stand for the pitch B flat. (Compound name.) N. B. These signs do not "*raise*" or "*lower*" notes, tones, pitches, letters or staff degrees.

11. *Double-sharp, Double-flat:* Given a staff with three or more degrees sharped in the signature, double-sharps are used (subject to the rules governing composition) to make certain of these degrees, already sharped, represent pitches one half-step higher yet. Similarly, when three or more degrees are flatted in the signature, double-flats are used to make certain degrees already flatted, represent pitches one half-step lower yet. Examples: To represent sharp 2 in the key of B major, double-sharp the C degree, or (equally good) double-sharp the third space (G clef). To represent flat 6 in the key of D flat major, double-flat the B degree, or (equally good) double flat the third line (G clef). *Do not say:* "Put a double-sharp on 6" or "put a double-sharp on C," or "*indicate* "a higher or lower pitch "*on*" a sharped or flatted degree.

12. *Signature:* Sharps or flats used as signatures affect the staff de-

---

[1] NOTE: — Not " space below the staff" or " space above the staff."

grees they occupy and all octaves of the same. Example: With signature of four sharps, the first one affects the fifth line and the first space; the second, the third space; the third, the space above and the second line; the fourth, the fourth line and the space below. *Do not say:* "F and C are sharped," "ti is sharped," "B is flatted," "fa is flatted." "Sharpened" or "flattened" are undesirable.

13. *Brace:* The two or more staffs containing parts to be sounded together; also the vertical line or bracket connecting such staffs. *Not* "line" or "score." "Staff" is better than "line" for a single staff, and "score" is used meaning the book containing an entire work, as "vocal score" "orchestral score," "full score."

14. *Notes:* Notes are characters designed to represent relative duration. When placed on staff-degrees they *indicate* pitch. (Note the difference between "represent" and "indicate.") "Sing what the note calls for" means, sing a tone of the pitch represented by the staff degree occupied by the note-head. The answer to the question: "What is that note?" would be "half-note," "eighth-note" according to the denomination of the note in question, whether it was on or off the staff.

15. *Measure-sign:* 4-4, 2-4, 6-8, are *measure-signs*. Avoid "time signatures," meter-signatures" "the fraction" "time-marks." Example: What is the measure-sign? (C) Ans. A broken circle. What is its meaning? Ans. Four-quarter measure. (Not four-four time, four-four rhythm, four-four meter.)

16. *Note Placing:* Place a quarter note on the fourth line. Not "put a quarter note on D."

17. *Beat-Pulse:* A tone or rest occurs on a certain beat or pulse of a measure. Not on a certain *count.*

18. *Signature Terminology:* The right hand sharp in the signature is on the staff degree that represents seven of the major scale. Not "always on 7 or ti."

19. *Signature Terminology:* The right hand flat in the signature is on the staff degree that represents four of the major scale. Not "always on fa."

20. *Rote, Note, Syllable:* Singing by rote means that the singer sings something learned by ear without regard to notes. Singing by note means that the singer is guided to the correct pitch by visible notes. Singing by syllable means that the singer sings the tones of a song or part to the sol-fa syllables instead of to words, neutral vowels or the hum. "Sing by note" is not correct if the direction means simply to sing the

sol-fa syllables, whether in sight reading, rote singing, or memory work. ".Sing by syllable" would be correct in each case.

ADOPTIONS OF THE 1911 MEETING AT SAN FRANCISCO

Arabic numerals, either 2, 3, 4, 5, 6, 9, or 12, placed on the staff directly after the signature and above the third line, show the number of beats in a measure.

A note, either a quarter or a dotted quarter, placed in parenthesis under the numeral, represents the length of one beat and is called the beat-note.

The numeral and the beat-note thus grouped constitute the measure-sign.

Illustrative statements covering proper terminology: the tune "America" is written in three-quarter measure. The chorus: "How lovely are the Messengers" is written in two-dotted quarter measure.

The above forms of statement were adopted at Denver in 1909, and are recommended for general use when speaking of music written with the conventional measure-signs, etc.

In place of: "two-two time, three-eight time, four-four time," say as above: "This piece is written in two-half measure, three-eighth measure, four-quarter measure."

MINOR SCALES

Primitive Minor (ascending)

The minor scale form having minor sixth and minor seventh above tonic to be called Primitive Minor.

Illustrative examples. A minor: a, b, c, d, e, f, g, a; C minor: c, d, e flat, f, g, a flat, b, c.

Primitive Minor (descending)

Same pitches in reverse order.

Harmonic Minor (ascending)

The minor scale form having minor sixth and major seventh above tonic to be called Harmonic Minor.

Illustrative examples. A minor: a b, c, d, e, f, g sharp, a; C minor: c, d, e flat, f, g, a flat, b, c.

Harmonic Minor (descending)

Same pitches in reverse order.

Melodic Minor (ascending)

The minor scale form having major sixth and major seventh above tonic to be called Melodic Minor.

Illustrative examples. A minor: a, b, c, d, e, f sharp, g sharp, a; C minor: c, d, e flat, f, g, a, b, c.

Melodic Minor (descending)

Same as the Primitive.

Adoptions of the 1912 Meeting at Chicago

Pulse and Beat

The Committee finds that the words: Pulse and Beat are in general use as synonymous terms, meaning one of the succession of throbs or impulses of which we are conscious when listening to music. Each of these pulses or beats has an exact point of beginning, a duration, and an exact point of ending, the latter coincident with the beginning of the next pulse or beat. When thus used, both words are terms of ear.

Beat

One of these words, Beat, is also in universal use, meaning one of a series of physical motions by means of which a conductor holds his group of performers to a uniform movement.

When thus used it becomes a term of eye.

The conductor's baton, if it is to be authoritative, cannot wander about through the whole duration of the pulse but must move quickly to a point of comparative repose, remaining until just before the arrival of the next pulse when it again makes a rapid swing, finishing coincidently with the initial tone (or silence) of the new pulse.

Thus it is practically the end of the conductor's beat that marks the beginning of the pulse.

The Committee is of opinion that Beat might preferably be used as indicating the outward sign.

Beat-Note

This term "beat-note" is already in use in another important connection (see Terminology Report, 1911) and the Committee recommends that those using the above terms shall say: "This note is an on-the-beat note; this one is an after-the-beat note; this one a before-the-beat note."

Definitions

Matters of Ear

Pulse: The unit of movement in music, one of a series of regularly recurring throbs or impulses.

Measure: A group of pulses.

Pulse-Group: Two or more tones grouped within the pulse.

Matters of Eye

Beat: One of a series of conventional movements made by the conductor. This might include any unconventional motion which served to mark the movement of the music, whether made by conductor, performer or auditor.

Beat-Note: A note of the denomination indicated by the measure-sign as the unit of note-value in a given measure.

Example

Given the following measure-signs: 2-4, 2-2, 2-8, quarter, half, or eighth notes, respectively, are beat-notes.

Beat-Group: A group of notes or notes and rests, of smaller denomination than the beat-note which represents a full beat from beginning to end and is equal in value to the beat-note. (A beat-group may begin with a rest.)

On-the-Beat Note (or rest): Any note (or rest) ranging in value from a full beat down, which calls for musical action (or inaction) synchronously with the conductor's beat.

After-the-Beat Note: Any note in a beat-group which indicates that a tone is to be sounded after the beginning, and before or at the middle of the pulse.

Before-the-Beat Note: Any note in a beat-group which indicates that a tone is to be sounded after the middle of the pulse.

To illustrate terminology and to differentiate between Pulse and Beat as terms, respectively of ear and eye, the following is submitted:

Whenever a brief tone involves the musical idea of syncopation, it may be regarded as an after-the-pulse tone and the note that calls for it as an after-the-beat note; when it involves the idea of anticipation or preparation it may be regarded as a before-the-pulse tone, and the note that calls for it, as a before-the-beat note.

Measure and Meter

"What is the measure-sign?"

"What is the meter-signature?"

These two words are used synonymously, and one of them is unnecessary. The Committee recommends that Measure be retained and used. Meter has its use in connection with hymns.

*   *   *   *   *   *   *   *   *   *   *   *

The author does not find it possible at present to agree with all the recommendations made in the above report, but the summary is printed in full for the sake of completeness.

The Music Teacher's National Association has also interested itself mildly in the subject of terminology reform, and at its meeting in Washington, D.C., in 1908, Professor Waldo S. Pratt gave his address as president of the Association on the subject "System and Precision in Musical Speech." This address interested the members of the Association to such an extent that Professor Pratt was asked to act as a committee whose purpose it should be to look into the matter of reforms necessary in music terminology and report at a later session. In 1910 Professor Pratt read a report in which he advocated the idea of making some changes in music nomenclature, but took the ground that the subject is too comprehensive to be mastered in the short time that can be given to it by a committee, and that it is therefore impossible to recommend specific changes. He also took occasion to remark that one difficulty in the whole matter of terminology is that many terms and expressions are used *colloquially* and that such use although usually not scientific, is often not distinctly harmful and is not of sufficient importance to cause undue excitement on the part of reformers. Quoting from the report at this point: — " A great deal of confusion is more apparent than real between *note* and *tone*, between *step* and *degree*, between *key* and *tonality*. No practical harm is done by speaking of the *first note* of a piece when really *first tone* would be more accurate. To say that a piece is written *in the key of Bb* is more convenient than to say that it is written in the *tonality of which Bb is the tonic*. The truth is that some of the niceties of expression upon which insistence is occasionally laid are merely fussy, not because they have not some sort of reason, but because they fail to take into account the practical difference between coloquial or off-hand speech and the diction of a scientific treatise. This is said without forgetting that colloquialism always needs watching and that some people form the habit of being careless or positively uncouth as if it were a mark of high artistic genius."

Professor Pratt's report is thus seen to be philosophic rather than constructive, and terminology reform will undoubtedly make more immediate progress through the efforts of the N. E. A. Committee with its specific recommendations (even though these are sometimes admittedly *fussy*) than through the policy of the M. T. N. A. of waiting for some one to get time to take up the subject in a scholarly way. Nevertheless the philosophic view is sometimes badly needed, especially when the spirit of reform becomes too rabid and attaches too great importance to trifles. A judicious intermingling of the two committees in a series of joint meetings would undoubtedly result in mutual helpfulness, and possibly also in a more tangible and convincing statement of principles than has yet been formulated by either.

APPENDIX E

Sonata Op. 31, No. 3 by Beethoven

Analysis by ARTHUR E. HEACOX,
Oberlin Conservatory of Music

First Subject 17 measures, E♭ major, as follows: 8 meas. presentation, one meas. link, 8 meas. repetition oct. higher. Rhythmic elements are A, B, C, all presented in first 8 meas.

1st Sub.

A   A rep.   B————   B rep.   C————

1   2   3   4   5   6   7

3   3   Linking measure.   A 8va

8   9   10

Ornament added.

A rep.   B   B   C

11   12   13   14   15   16

A ornament added.

End of 1st Sub.   A   A rep. in ribattuta.

Rhythm   1st Episode.*   B
(Bridge   to 2d Sub)

17   18   19   20   21

overlapping rhythm of bass B in diminution.

* The Episode has three divisions, 1st div. meas 18–25, 2nd div. 25–32, 3d div. 33–45.

* A device in instrumental music whereby a phrase of two notes is accelerated, even to the extent of becoming a trill.

F from Seiten-Thema 28–32.
D
49
50
51
12
Link of four measures.
52
53
54
55
56
D
var.
D rep.
var.
E var.
57
58
59
D
var.
F var.
60
61
62
2nd Episode, 19 meas.
(or Closing Group.)
might be
termed G.
tr
variant of meas. 8.
var. of D.
63
64
65

G see 65
G
G
G
64, 65, 8va.
Cross rhythm.
From C, see meas. 26; 16ths becoming 8ths.
See meas. 9
A, enlarged.
Codetta 6 meas. G var.
82 rep.
A
A
Development
48 meas.
A rep.
B
B rep.
B rep.
Modulating.
A

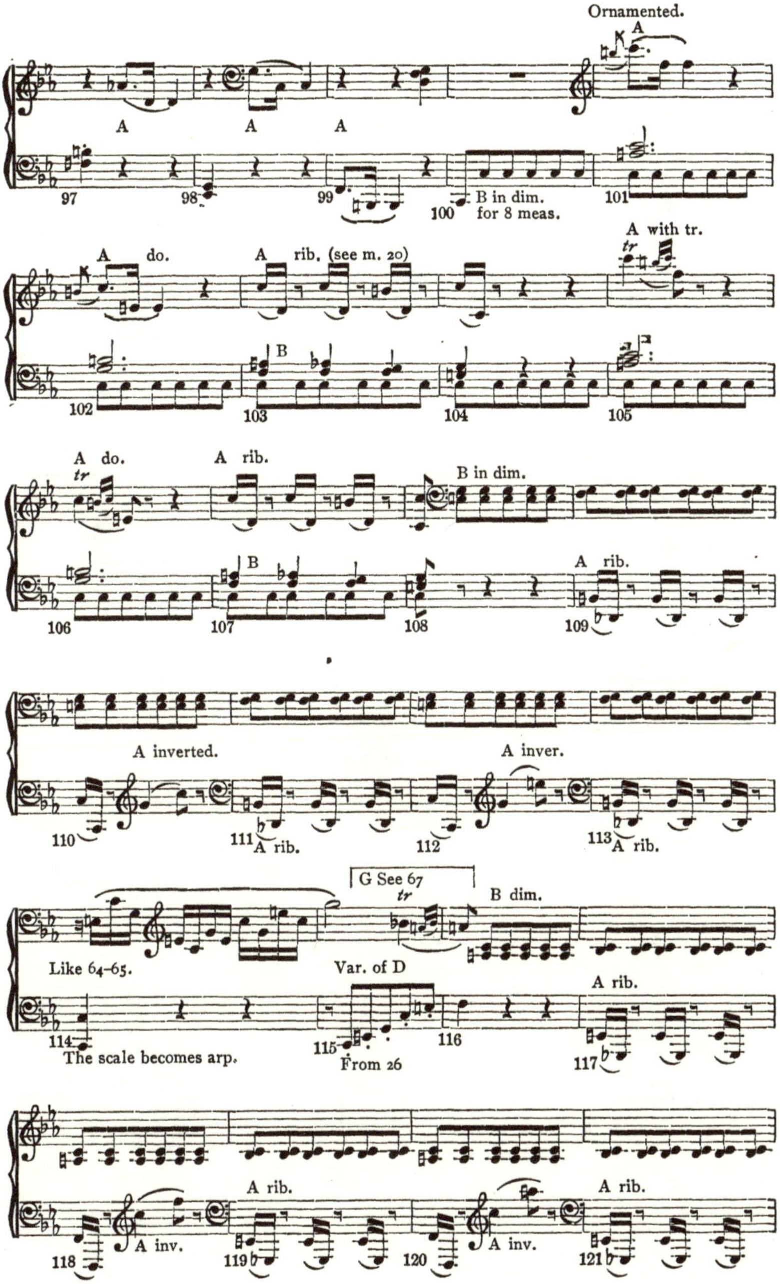
Ornamented.
A
A
A
A
97
98
99
100
B in dim.
for 8 meas.
101
A do.
A rib. (see m. 20)
A with tr.
tr
B
102
103
104
105
A do.
tr
A rib.
B in dim.
B
A rib.
106
107
108
109
A inverted.
A inver.
110
111
A rib.
112
113
A rib.
G See 67
tr
B dim.
Like 64–65.
Var. of D
A rib.
114
The scale becomes arp.
115
From 26
116
117
A rib.
A rib.
A inv.
A inv.
118
119
120
121

G
meas. 114-115 rep. higher.
Again rep. higher still.
122
123
124
G
again rep. still dif. hight.
G
G inver.
G inver.
interval expan.
125
126
127
128
129
G inver.
int. ex.
int. ex.
Cross rhythm.
130
131
132
133
134
135
Recapitulation
A
A rep.
B
B rep.
or Reprise.
Exact for 17 meas.
136
137
138
139
140
141
142
C
A
143
144
145
146
A rep. orna.
C
End of 1st Sub.
B
B rep.
1st Episode.
147
148
149
150
151
152
153
Overlapping rhythm.

A
A
A rib. (see meas. 20)
16 meas. Not a bridge this time.
B
154
155
156
157
Var. of meas. 22, 23, 24.
B
158
159
160
161 to 167 like 25-31.
161
162
163
164
Part of original bridge omitted.
165
166
167
168
169
D
D rep.
2nd Sub. 20 meas. E♭ maj.
E
170
171
172
D
F see meas. 51.
173
174
175

Link expanded from four bars to six adding brilliancy.

176 177

178 179 180

cf. 53-56.

D var.

181 182 183

D var. E var.

184 185 186

D var. F var.

187 188 189

End. 2nd
Sub.

G
tr

Var. of D. See 65. 190-191 8va Cross
2nd Episode (or closing Gr.) rhythm

G
tr

190 Var. of meas. 8. 191 192 193
Overlapping rhythm.

Thirteen appearances of G instead of seven.

Compare 72 to 82.
From C.

One measure added. (See 75–77.)

Codetta. compare 82–87.
6 meas.

Coda.   A rep.

A Terminal development   B

rib. dismembered.
B
B
B
B
C
meas. 8–9 chromatic.
A
A
B
B
B rib.
chromatic passage. (See 235–236.)
246–249. compare 25–28.
compare 72–74.
B rib.

INDEX

Also from Benediction Books ...
Wandering Between Two Worlds: Essays on Faith and Art
Anita Mathias
Benediction Books, 2007
152 pages
ISBN: 0955373700

Available from www.amazon.com, www.amazon.co.uk

In these wide-ranging lyrical essays, Anita Mathias writes, in lush,
lovely prose, of her naughty Catholic childhood in Jamshedpur, India;
her large, eccentric family in Mangalore, a sea-coast town converted
by the Portuguese in the sixteenth century; her rebellion and atheism
as a teenager in her Himalayan boarding school, run by German mis-
sionary nuns, St. Mary's Convent, Nainital; and her abrupt religious
conversion after which she entered Mother Teresa's convent in Calcut-
ta as a novice. Later rich, elegant essays explore the dualities of her
life as a writer, mother, and Christian in the United States-- Domestici-
ty and Art, Writing and Prayer, and the experience of being "an alien
and stranger" as an immigrant in America, sensing the need for roots.

About the Author

Anita Mathias is the author of *Wandering Between Two Worlds: Essays on Faith and Art*. She has a B.A. and M.A. in English from
Somerville College, Oxford University, and an M.A. in Creative Writing from the Ohio State University, USA. Anita won a National
Endowment of the Arts fellowship in Creative Nonfiction in 1997.
She lives in Oxford, England with her husband, Roy, and her daugh-
ters, Zoe and Irene.

Anita's website:
   http://www.anitamathias.com, and
Anita's blog Dreaming Beneath the Spires:
   http://dreamingbeneaththespires.blogspot.com

The Church That Had Too Much
Anita Mathias
Benediction Books, 2010
52 pages
ISBN: 9781849026567

Available from www.amazon.com, www.amazon.co.uk

The Church That Had Too Much was very well-intentioned. She
wanted to love God, she wanted to love people, but she was both hampered by her muchness and the abundance of her possessions, and
beset by ambition, power struggles and snobbery. Read about the sur-
prising way The Church That Had Too Much began to resolve her
problems in this deceptively simple and enchanting fable.

About the Author

Anita Mathias is the author of *Wandering Between Two Worlds: Es-*
says on Faith and Art. She has a B.A. and M.A. in English from
Somerville College, Oxford University, and an M.A. in Creative Writing from the Ohio State University, USA. Anita won a National
Endowment of the Arts fellowship in Creative Nonfiction in 1997.
She lives in Oxford, England with her husband, Roy, and her daugh-
ters, Zoe and Irene.

Anita's website:
    http://www.anitamathias.com, and
Anita's blog Dreaming Beneath the Spires:
    http://dreamingbeneaththespires.blogspot.com